Life after Death

Life after Death

Christianity's Hope and Challenge

DICK TRIPP

Foreword by Derek Eaton

WIPF & STOCK · Eugene, Oregon

LIFE AFTER DEATH
Christianity's Hope and Challenge

Copyright © 2015 Dick Tripp. All rights reserved. Except for brief quotations in critical publications or reviews, no part of this book may be reproduced in any manner without prior written permission from the publisher. Write: Permissions. Wipf and Stock Publishers, 199 W. 8th Ave., Suite 3, Eugene, OR 97401.

Wipf and Stock
An Imprint of Wipf and Stock Publishers
199 W. 8th Ave., Suite 3
Eugene, OR 97401

www.wipfandstock.com

ISBN 13: 978-1-62564-243-1

Manufactured in the U.S.A.   01/05/2015

Unless otherwise noted, Bible quotations are taken from the New International Version. Copyright 1978 by the New York International Bible Society.

Scripture quotations marked (CEV) are from the Contemporary English Version. Copyright © 1991, 1992, 1995 by American Bible Society. Used by Permission.

Contents

Foreword by Derek Eaton | vii
Preface | ix

Part 1: Exploring the Territory
1 Why It Matters What We Believe | 3
2 The Avoidance of Death in Our Modern World | 16
3 The Reasonableness of Life after Death | 20

Part 2: The Christian View of Life after Death
4 The Nature of Christian Conversion | 31
5 Resurrection, Not Reincarnation | 35
6 Between Death and Resurrection | 52
7 The Nature of Heaven | 54
8 Stories of Faith | 75
9 What about Judgment? | 93
10 The Future of Unbelievers | 105
11 A Choice to Be Made | 121

Appendices | 127
Looking for the Sunrise | 128
Treasure Up in Heaven | 130
A Traveller's Guide to Heaven | 132
Heaven | 135
Hamish | 137

The King and the Fool | 139
Will You Meet Me at the Fountain? | 140

Bibliography | 141

Foreword

In every age death has held a perennial fascination for men and women, and there is a plethora of ideas about death and especially what lies beyond—every religion has its philosophy on the matter. However, biblical Christianity is unique in what it claims happens after we die.

Life beyond death is, I believe, an essential part of the good news God has revealed in Jesus Christ. Moreover, it is a part of Christian teaching that has become increasingly neglected over recent decades. There is widespread misunderstanding of what science and technology do and do not say in this area. We have, in the West, had a priceless treasure stolen from us without realizing it. This has led to a lack of assurance and understanding of God's provision and keeping power in many lives.

How can we know about such things? Is your guess as good a mine? In this age of pluralism can we know the truth?

Dick Tripp, in this excellent, helpful and timely volume, leads us to the Christian's source book—the Bible—for meaningful answers. Answers that underscore once again what a loving, caring God we have who has made every provision that we could ever need for this life and for eternity.

Derek Eaton, QSM, MA, Dip Theol
Formerly Bishop of Nelson, New Zealand,
and Assistant Bishop of Cairo

Preface

The purpose of this booklet is to look in some depth at the important issues surrounding death. In part 1, I will look at questions such as: Does it matter what we believe anyway? Why do we avoid talking about it? Can we confidently assume that there is life after death? In part 2, I will present the Christian view of death and what lies beyond. I won't avoid the difficult question of judgment and the possibility of missing out on all that God has planned for his people, issues that the New Testament speaks so plainly and consistently about. However, for those who are searching for a real relationship with the living God, I have a glorious message of hope and certainty. You don't have to go through life with any doubt about the future. On the contrary, if you are willing to accept all that God offers, on his terms, you will be able to look forward with certainty to an endless future in which you will experience all that God, in his infinite love and wisdom, has planned for you. You will also find it a hope that will transform your goals and values and understanding of every part of this present life. My prayer is that you will be greatly blessed as you make the journey.

Part 1

Exploring the Territory

A fire-and-brimstone cleric visiting a country church began his sermon with the stirring reminder, "Everybody in this parish is going to die." He was discomforted to notice a man in the front pew grinning broadly. "Why are you so amused?" he asked. "I'm not in this parish," replied the man. "I'm just visiting my sister for the weekend."

The subject of death, what it means and what may or may not lie beyond, is not a popular subject in our Western society. We may joke about it, but that may well hide our unease. George Bernard Shaw once observed that the statistics about death are very impressive—one out of one dies. We can certainly be optimistic if we wish. *The Jewish Chronicle* recorded an account of a 103-year-old Jewish woman living in Ramat Gan, Israel. She was looking for a suitable husband for herself, and in her optimism, stated that in the event of her becoming a widow after marriage, she would make no financial demands on her husband's family. However, even her life must come to an end. Charles Kettering said, "My interest is in the future because I am going to spend the rest of my life there." That makes a lot of sense. So let's begin the journey by exploring some of the reasons why this subject of life after death is important.

1

Why It Matters What We Believe
I would suggest three main reasons.

THE SHORTNESS AND UNCERTAINTY OF LIFE

Seventy years or more may seem a very long time from our perspective—that is, until we start approaching the end. However, if it should be true that there is life after death and that the future life has no end, then the span of our present existence is infinitesimal in comparison. The Bible constantly reminds us of the shortness of this life, viewed from God's perspective. It speaks of our life as a shadow that passes (Job 8:9), swifter than a runner (Job 9:25), as grass that withers and a flower that falls (1 Pet 1:24), and as a mist that appears for a little while and then vanishes (Jas 4:14). The Psalmist was wise to pray, "Teach us to number our days aright, that we may gain a heart of wisdom" (Ps 90:12).

Seldom a day passes without some reminder that, as the hymn states, "the crib and the coffin are carved from the self-same tree."[1] And none of us knows when the end will come. An old English proverb states that the young may die, but the old must

---

1. Houghton, "By Life, or By Death."

die.² We rightly express sadness or horror when tragedy or evil take innocent lives, particularly in youth, but we easily forget, as C. S. Lewis is purported to have said, that "war does not increase death—death is total in every generation."[3] Even if we are fortunate to make it through the "seven ages of man"—spills, drills, thrills, bills, ills, pills and wills—the end will come soon enough. What then?

Author William Saroyan, who once wrote that "the best part of a man stays for ever," died in May 1981 after a two-year battle with cancer. Only five days before he entered hospital in April, he telephoned the Associated Press to report that cancer had spread to several of his vital organs. He then gave this final statement to be used after his death: "Everybody has got to die, but I have always believed an exception would be made in my case. Now what?"[4] The Bible declares, "People are destined to die once, and after that to face judgment" (Heb 9:27). If that is true, then it will be very sad if we discover we have left it too late to face up to the issues involved. It is significant that Jesus described as a fool the person who invests all their hopes in this life and does not take into account the fact that at any time they may be called to meet their Creator (Luke 12:20).

TODAY'S LIFESTYLE SHAPED BY VIEW OF AFTERLIFE

It has been customary for some who would ridicule the Christian view of heaven to speak of "pie in the sky when you die." However, as theologian Alister McGrath points out in his book on suffering, that taunt evades the question of whether it is true. "If the Christian hope of heaven is an illusion, based upon lies, then it must be abandoned as misleading and deceitful. But if it is true, it must be

---

2. See Speake, *Oxford Dictionary of Proverbs*, 77.
3. Quoted in Graham, *Death and the Life After*, 3.
4. Associated Press, "Saroyan Telephoned His Final Statement," *Eugene (Oregon) Register-Guard*, May 1981.

embraced and allowed to transfigure our entire understanding of the place of suffering in life."⁵

Not only will it transfigure our understanding of the meaning of suffering, but also our goals, our values, our relationships, our attitude to material possessions, our handling of crises and grief, and our overall enjoyment of this life.

In literature (and television) there is a story, which has been told in a number of different ways. It is the story of a man who opens a newspaper and discovers that the date on the newspaper is six months in advance of the time in which he lives. He reads through the paper and discovers stories about events that have not yet taken place. On the financial page he comes across a report of the rise and fall of various stocks and bonds. Instantly he recognizes that this knowledge can make him a wealthy man. He is delighted. Turning the page he comes across the obituary column. There he sees his picture and story. Suddenly everything changes. The knowledge of his impending death immediately changes his views about wealth.

In a perceptive chapter in *I Was Just Wondering*, titled "Imagine There's No Heaven," well-known writer Philip Yancey describes what society might look like if it did not believe in any afterlife. With apologies to Samuel Butler, author of *Erehwon*, he calls this society "Acirema" (America spelled backwards). He suggests the following scenario:

1) *Youth is valued above all else.* Sports are a national obsession. Magazine covers present wrinkle-free faces and gorgeous bodies. Best-selling videos are those that demonstrate exercises which can make you look a decade younger.

2) *Old age is not valued.* It is a distasteful reminder of the end of life. Skin creams, cosmetic surgery and other elaborate means are promoted to mask the effects of ageing. The elderly are confined in their own housing, shut away from the general populace.

---

5. McGrath, *Suffering*, 100–101.

Part 1: Exploring the Territory

3) *"Image" is emphasized rather than "substance."* Practices that demonstrate achievement in this life are valued over inner qualities such as compassion, self-sacrifice and humility. The disabled and disfigured have a hard time competing.

4) *Acireman religion focuses exclusively on how one fares in the here and now.* Those who still believe in a God look for his approval in terms of good health and prosperity on earth.

5) *Crime has taken a turn toward the violent and bizarre.* Without a vague fear of eternal judgment hanging over them, Aciremans have no deterrents to such behavior.

6) *Billions of dollars are spent on life support systems while at the same time abortion is strongly encouraged.* This is not as paradoxical as it seems, for Aciremans believe that human life begins at birth and ends at death.

7) *"Acceptance" rather than fear or anger is viewed as the most mature response to death.* Scholars devalue ancient attitudes about dying a "noble" or confrontational death. The ideal death is a peaceful departure during sleep.

8) *Much effort is put into eliminating the problem of death.* Scientists are working on it. Death takes place in sealed-off areas in the presence of trained professionals. Terms such as "passing" and "going on" are substituted for the inelegant word "death." Ceremonies play down its discontinuity from life.[6]

Does that sound familiar?

In contrast to this, those who have found confidence from their relationship with God that they will spend eternity in a love relationship with him will tend toward the following values:

1) *Wealth is seen as an opportunity for service.* "Command those who are rich in this present world . . . to do good, to be rich in good deeds, and to be generous and willing to share. In this way they will lay up treasure for themselves as a firm foundation for the coming age, so that they may take hold of the life

---

6. Yancey, *I Was Just Wondering*, 216–17.

that is truly life" (1 Tim 6:17–19). The emphasis is on laying up treasure in heaven, not on earth (Matt 6:19–21).

2) *Character is given priority over success and popularity.* As Ravi Zacharias puts it in *A Shattered Visage*, "Death is the one experience when we leave behind everything we have and take with us everything we are."[7] A similar statement was made by the South African cricketer Jonty Rhodes. He was named Wisden Cricketer of the year in 1999 and was recently appointed patron of the World Cup volunteers program. They were looking for someone who would be a good role model, and Jonty was their unanimous choice. He has committed his life to Christ and has a long-term perspective. In an article in *Challenge Weekly*, he said, "I realise now that success didn't depend on me scoring a hundred, or taking catches or getting run-outs. I want to be the best I can for my God. Whatever you gain, or records you attain, they are going to be left behind. It's what you've got in your heart that's going to be taken with you."[8]

As Jesus underlined in the Sermon on the Mount, those who are truly blessed are those who have manifested a goodness of character, especially those for whom it has brought suffering and ridicule (Matt 5:2–12). Their goodness will be rewarded (Matt 25:34–36).

3) *Suffering is seen as a means of developing character, strengthening faith and providing opportunities for ministry to others.* Consider, for instance, the following passages from the New Testament: "We gladly suffer, because we know that suffering helps us to endure. And endurance builds character, which gives us a hope that will never disappoint us. All of this happens because God has given us the Holy Spirit, who fills our hearts with his love" (Rom 5:3–5 CEV). "These trials will prove that your faith is worth much more than gold that can

---

7. Zacharias, *Shattered Visage*, 94.

8. *Challenge Weekly* was a New Zealand Christian paper that has ceased publication.

be destroyed. They will show that you will be given praise and honor and glory when Jesus Christ returns" (1 Pet 1:7 CEV). "The Father is a merciful God, who always gives us comfort. He comforts us when we are in trouble, so that we can share that same comfort with others in trouble" (2 Cor 1:3–4 CEV).

Suffering and trials can also be seen as a means of focusing our attention on the things that will last and where true and lasting joys are to be found. Elisabeth Elliot's first husband gave his life attempting to bring the gospel to the Auca Indians in South America, and she has since lost two husbands to cancer. Her books and public ministry have brought encouragement and guidance to many. In *Keep a Quiet Heart*, she writes, "Heaven is not here, it's There. If we were given all we wanted here, our hearts would settle for this world rather than the next. God is forever luring us up and away from this one, wooing us to Himself and His still invisible Kingdom, where we will certainly find what we so keenly long for."[9] As I have heard said, suffering swells our feet so that earth's shoes don't fit.

4) *Priority is given to those things that will last.* The most important things in this life are those that outlast it. Or as C. S. Lewis put it, "All that is not eternal is eternally out of date."[10] That is why the New Testament puts so much emphasis on love as the greatest of virtues. God's purpose in creation was that we should live in eternal love relationships with him and with others. Paul finishes his great chapter on love (1 Cor 13) by speaking of the things that will last beyond this life: "Love never fails . . . Now we see but a poor reflection; then we shall see face to face . . . Now these three remain: faith, hope and love. But the greatest of these is love" (vv. 8–13).

In his wonderful little book on this chapter, *The Greatest Thing in the World*, Henry Drummond says,

---

9. Elliot, *Keep a Quiet Heart*, 28.
10. Lewis, *Four Loves*, 125.

I have enjoyed almost every pleasure that he has planned for man; and yet as I look back I see standing out above all the life that has gone, four or five short experiences when the love of God reflected itself in some poor imitation, some small act of love of mine, and these seem to be the very things which alone of all one's life abide. Everything else in all our lives is transitory. Every other good is visionary. But the acts of love which no man knows about, or can ever know about—they never fail.[11]

5) *The eternal security that is found in a relationship with God through Jesus will enable believers to take risks for the kingdom of God.* Because we have a secure hope for the future we can rise above things that tend to bind us to this present existence such as success, wealth, power or security (which is only temporary anyway). We are free to take risks for the kingdom God. As God has guaranteed our future we can become pioneering agents for change, challenging suffering, ignorance, discrimination and injustice. David Neff, in an article in *Christianity Today*, relates this to the example of William Wilberforce, who risked his reputation and fortune in his fight against the slave trade.[12]

Paul speaks of God as the "God of hope" and says that Christians should "overflow with hope by the power of the Holy Spirit" (Rom 15:13). Commenting on this verse, in his impressive volume *God's Empowering Presence*, Gordon Fee says,

> Here Paul prays that they may live in the Spirit in such a way that they overflow with the confidence that is theirs as to their certain future. Such 'future-oriented' people live in the present in a way different from the rest—not as "too heavenly minded to be of any earthly good," but as so confident of the future that they can pour themselves into the present with utter abandon, full of joy and peace, because nothing in the present can ultimately

---

11. Drummond, *Greatest Thing in the World*, 60–61.
12. Neff, "Honest Appraisal."

overwhelm them. Such people make the Christian faith a truly attractive alternative.[13]

The popular writer A. W. Tozer expressed a similar thought: "When the followers of Jesus Christ lose their interest in heaven they will no longer be happy Christians, and when they are no longer happy Christians they cannot be a powerful force in a sad and sinful world."[14]

6) *People are valued because they are created for fellowship with God, are loved by him and have at least the potential for an eternal existence in his kingdom.* For these reasons, all humans have value regardless of physical or mental capabilities, age or culture. People matter more than things, which will pass away. This has relevance to issues such as abortion, euthanasia and justice.

7) *Life will have a lot more meaning and purpose.* According to one study, 51 percent of women aged between twenty and thirty-five feel bored or hopeless when thinking about the future. However, even when earthly things look pretty grim, Christians who know where they are going and are living for eternity know that there is always light at the end of the tunnel. They have something to live for that will last forever.

8) *It will put a totally new perspective on many of the trials and problems we face in life.* A. W. Tozer wrote, "The man who comes to a right belief about God is relieved of 10,000 temporal problems, for he sees at once that these have to do with matters which, at the most, cannot concern him for very long."[15]

This is how Wing Commander Bransome Burbridge, who won two DSOs and two DFCs for his night fighter exploits over Germany during World War II, described the experience of his first dogfight:

---

13. Fee, *God's Empowering Presence*, 623.
14. Tozer, *Who Put Jesus on the Cross?*, 105.
15. Tozer, *Knowledge of the Holy*, 10–11.

> In our first real scrap our opponent seemed to be outturning me; I turned tighter than ever and banked very steeply—this "toppled" the instruments which would take twenty minutes to reset themselves, so even if he didn't get us first we might spin into the sea . . . I felt prickly—I was afraid. Then something hit me but I realised it wasn't a bullet. In a split second . . . I realised two things; both stemmed from the fact that I was a Christian. First, if God had further work for me to do for him after the War I was bound to survive; second, if I did get killed, death would be literally the gateway to heaven and I should see the Lord Jesus Christ, so what did it matter.

He continued reflectively:

> I have not been afraid of death since then, but it took a dogfight over Germany to make me see this. When I leave this earth I shall live eternal life in Christ's presence. Whilst I am here I live it "at a distance." Through it he has taught me so many lessons, guided me through so many problems, given me so much satisfaction, spoken to me so often, that my belief in the living Christ would never be destroyed. Try telling the pilot at an overseas station that the R.A.F. does not exist—and he'll tell you you are talking through your helmet.[16]

9) *Death, though still an enemy (1 Cor 15:26), is a defeated foe and can be faced with confidence, even joy.* Prominent German theologian Helmut Thielicke observed that the New Testament exhibits near contempt for it. Consider the following passages: "Christ our Savior has defeated death and brought us the good news. It shines like a light and offers life that never ends" (2 Tim 1:10 CEV). The sting of death (fear of judgment) has been removed by the cross. "Sin is what gives death its sting, and the Law is the power behind sin. But thank God for letting our Lord Jesus Christ give us the victory!" (1 Cor 15:56–57 CEV). "Since the children have flesh and blood, he too shared in their humanity so that by his death he might

---

16. From Rawnsley and Wright, *Night Fighter*.

Part 1: Exploring the Territory

destroy him who holds the power of death—that is, the devil—and free those who all their lives were held in slavery by their fear of death" (Heb 2:14–15). The New Testament uses different phrases to describe the death of those who belong to Christ. It is to "sleep in Jesus" (1 Thess 4:14), "to depart and to be with Christ" (Phil 1:23), to put off a suit of clothes in order "to be clothed with our heavenly dwelling" (2 Cor 5:1–4), to go home to be with the Lord (2 Cor 5:8), to depart on a journey (2 Tim 4:6–8), to "rest from . . . labor" (Rev 14:13). As the great Baptist preacher Charles Spurgeon put it, "Death is the loosing of the cable that the bark may freely sail to the fair havens. Death is the fiery chariot in which we ascend to God: it is the voice of the Great King, who comes into his banqueting hall, and says, 'Friend, come up higher.'"[17] For the Christian, it is the putting away of the feeble lamp, because the dawn has come.

Christians have a great advantage when facing death, through their relationship with Jesus, the one who himself has made that journey and understands it fully. Philip Yancey, in his wonderful book *The Jesus I Never Knew*, tells of a doctor who said to him, "When my patients pray, they are talking to someone who has actually died—something that's not true of any other adviser, counsellor, or death expert."[18]

Later we will explore these themes more. For someone with this perspective, even the suffering caused by terminal illness can be transformed. Wendy Bray is the author of *In the Palm of God's Hand*—her prayer diaries following the first year of her life with cancer—for which she won the biography category of the Christian Book Awards in 2002. She has said that we have, in many ways, lost our eternal perspective, but that the Christian life is more about the next life than about this one. As Helmut Thielicke points out, there is a significant difference between regarding death as a leaving of this earthly existence, and regarding it as going to where

---

17. Spurgeon, "Christ the Destroyer of Death," in *Sermons on Death*, 565.
18. Yancey, *Jesus I Never Knew*, 271.

we ultimately belong. If we say that we have to "depart," then the values and the things that we are leaving behind are our frame of reference. But if we can say that we're "going home," then all of that diminishes, and we ultimately come to see only the home where we are headed. Some people believe in heaven. Others look forward to it!

Taking our stand in eternity gives us leverage to use in this life. Martin Luther King Jr. said we should live with one foot in the air. Where those of us who claim to be Christian do not appear to be living by these values, part of the reason must surely be because we do not have a clear enough vision of eternal realities. We are living too much as citizens of earth rather than the citizens of heaven that we are (Phil 3:20–21). Well-known theologian James Packer complains that we have lost the Puritans' great sense that we should "regard readiness to die as the first step in learning to live."[19] It is not that we are too heavenly minded, but not heavenly minded enough. If we are to make a real difference in this world then we must "set [our] hearts on things above" (Col 3:1–4). Of course, this doesn't mean that we spend all our time thinking about heaven. Ron Hay, in an article in *Latimer* magazine, makes a pertinent point: "It seems to me that we are called not so much to be heavenly-minded as to be heavenly-hearted. The athlete has his heart (his desire) fixed on a gold medal, but he doesn't spend all day-dreaming about the medal. His mind is on training schedules, times, diet, in short on how to get the medal. So we must have our heart set on heaven and our minds set on working out our salvation and service in this world."[20]

C. S. Lewis pointed out that if you study history, you will find that those who have made the greatest difference in this life are those who have thought most highly of the next. Some things are even worth dying for. And, as Professor Oliver O'Donovan

---

19. Packer, *Quest for Godliness*, 13.
20. Hay, "Christian Hope," *Latimer*, January, 1987, 11.

Part 1: Exploring the Territory

observed, "No good can be worth dying for unless there is a heavenly good that is worth living for."[21]

Whatever we believe about death and what lies beyond, it will vitally affect the meaning we give to this life and how we choose to live it. The widely respected United Nations general secretary Dag Hammarskjöld, according to James Packer, "was thinking Christianly when he wrote that no philosophy that cannot make sense of death can make sense of life either . . . No one's living will be right until these truths about death are anchored in his or her heart."[22]

THE POSSIBILITY OF MISSING OUT ON ALL GOD HAS PLANNED FOR YOU

A third reason why our beliefs about the future life are so important is because of the possibility that everything Jesus taught about judgment beyond death may be true. As I shall explore later, the New Testament is very explicit and consistent in its teaching that not everyone is going to make it into God's future. It is also very explicit about what we must do to be assured of a place in it. Whatever we believe about the future of those who do miss out, it would be a tragic mistake to delay our search for the truth until death has crept up on us, either in old age or sooner.

Billy Graham was once speaking to University of California students at a Campus Crusade evangelistic convention. The radicals in the audience interrupted parts of his message with boos and catcalls, but they quieted down when he spoke of their unresolved problems—death and eternity. He told about a college student who was fatally injured in a car accident. Her last words to her mother were these: "Mother, you taught me everything I needed to know to get by in college. You taught me how to light my cigarette, how to hold my cocktail glass, and how to have intercourse safely. But

---

21. Quoted by George Carey, "Gospel as Public Truth," conference address, 14 July 1992.
22. Packer, *God's Plans for You*, 203.

Mother, you never taught me how to die. You better teach me quickly, Mother, because I'm dying."[23]

If God longs for us to be reconciled to him as much as the Bible says he does, he will not deny us if we are genuinely sincere in our search. "You will find him if you look for him with all your heart and with all your soul" (Deut 4:29).

---

23. Quoted by Caldwell, *Another Tassel Is Moved*, 56.

2

The Avoidance of Death in Our Modern World

If we are agreed that the matter is of some importance, why is it that we avoid talking about it? Helmut Thielicke observed that death is coming to have the same position in modern life and literature that sex had in Victorian times. One of the best descriptions of the modern attitude toward death that I have come across is given by philosopher and social commentator Os Guiness in *The Dust of Death*. He says,

> Contemporary society . . . meets death by escaping into romanticism. It was once a common idea that when Christian views of death, dying and the afterlife were removed, there could be a new, free, pragmatic, almost casual approach to death, one releasing man from the fear of non-being. The reverse is the case, partially because of the aggravation of twentieth-century social problems and the addition of the Eastern concept of reincarnation, but especially because men cannot escape the fear of non-being. Secular man now has an even greater fear of death and non-being. The gross commercialism of grief and dying is only the flip side of the fear of death; the fear

is hiding itself in an extreme romanticism, laying men open to manipulation.[1]

There are many ways of avoiding the subject. In a *Time* magazine article, "On Death as a Constant Companion," psychologist Rollo May said, "We run away from death by making a cult of automatic process or by making it impersonal. Many people think they are facing death when they are really side stepping it with the old 'eat, drink and be merry, for tomorrow you die'—middle-aged men and women who want to love everybody, go every place, do everything, and hear everything before the end comes. It is like the advertising slogan 'If I have only one life . . . let me live it as a blonde.'"

He points to our modern-day obsession with sex as one of the ways we avoid facing death: "The clamour of sex drowns out the ever-waiting presence of death . . . Death is the symbol of ultimate impotence and finiteness. What would we see if we cut though our obsession with sex? That we must die."[2]

The fact that we do not talk about death does not mean that we do not *think* about it. A team of psychiatrists in Missouri came to the conclusion, on the basis of tests that indicate what goes on under the skin and inside the skulls of Americans of all ages, that people think four-and-a-half times as much about how to solve the riddle of death and what comes after it as they do about sex and romance. Similarly, an opinion poll among three thousand West German teenagers in Kitzingen, only 5 percent of whom belonged to church youth groups, revealed that the number-one question on their minds concerned life after death. Social and political questions, which the pollsters (public school religious teachers) expected to rank higher, interested them less.

In his Pulitzer Prize–winning book *The Denial of Death*, Ernest Becker suggested that the primary concern of every living person is death, and most people deal with that concern by

---

1. Guinness, *Dust of Death*, 33.
2. Quoted in May, "On Death," *Time*, November 12, 1965.

denying that it will ever happen to them.[3] That reminds me of a story told of a certain Lord Palmerston. Seriously ill, his doctor told him the severity of the situation. He huffily replied, "Die, my dear doctor! That is the last thing I shall do!"

Many who do not believe in life after death, or at least are uncertain on that score, are prepared to face it with a stoical courage. Billy Graham, referencing Eugene O'Neill's *Long Day's Journey into Night*, suggests that O'Neill's philosophical attitude typifies that of our age: "Life's only meaning is death . . . so face it with courage and even love of the inevitable. Death becomes like a blanket on a cold night."[4] However, you don't have to scratch people very hard to find that not far beneath the surface there is an anxiety about death, even a real fear. Melanie Klein, an English psychoanalyst, believed fear of death is at the root of all human anxiety. Paul Tillich, the renowned theologian, based his theory of anxiety on the idea that man is finite and must die. Austrian psychiatrist William Stekel went so far as to express the hypothesis that every fear we have is ultimately fear of death.[5]

However, it is not just the thought of annihilation that causes us to fear death. Epicurus, the Greek philosopher, believed that what many fear is not that death is annihilation, but that it is not, and there may be an unpleasant afterwards.[6] If it is indeed true that we live in a moral universe, and that our moral awareness does not just come from some evolutionary process, but behind everything is a God of moral perfection who has created us with a moral conscience, then that puts a certain perspective on things. If, as the Bible consistently states, we are accountable to God and one day we will have to give an account of what we have done with our lives, and if we will ultimately be judged by God's standards, and

---

3. Becker, *Denial of Death*, xvii.
4. Graham, *World Aflame*, 60.
5. See Friedman, *Encyclopedia of Mental Health*, 438.
6. Cited by Green, *Man Alive!*, 79.

not ours, then maybe we have every right to be afraid of death.[7] It is only the most callous (or dishonest!) who are not conscious of their failures in this respect. James Packer puts this bluntly: "Physical death is the outward sign of that eternal separation from God which is the creator's judgment on sin, and which will only become deeper and more painful through the milestone event of dying, unless saving grace intervenes. Unconverted people do well therefore to fear death: it is in truth fearsome."[8]

Avoidance of death, however, has its consequences. Joseph Bayly, whose three sons pre-deceased him, wrote, "When a civilisation denies death and hems its members in with cars and amusements, science and organ transplants, against the mystical elements of life that reach their zenith in death, we should not be surprised if young men and women create their own mystery through conscious-expanding drugs and Eastern religions. Nor perhaps, should we be surprised if that civilisation has a high rate of mental illness and suicide."[9]

Paul Helm adds, "Because death is often associated with deep grief and an acute sense of loss, it is sugar-coated, or even plastic-coated, the perfect vehicle for inducing superstition."[10]

Christianity has an answer to all of this, but before exploring the Bible's outlook, there is one other subject I wish to tackle—is it *reasonable* to believe in life after death, and the two options that the Bible describes?

---

7. I have explored this theme in some depth in the booklet *Does It Matter How We Live? A Christian View of Morality*. It can be read on www.christianity.co.nz or www.exploringchristianity.com.

8. Packer, "Dying Well Is the Final Test," *Eternity*, January 1987.

9. Bayly, *View from the Hearse*.

10. Helm, *Last Things*, 35–36.

3

The Reasonableness of Life after Death

Of course, not everyone believes in life after death. H. J. Blackham, in *Objections to Humanism*, said, "On humanist ideals life leads to nothing and every pretence that it does not is a deceit."[1] There are, however, plenty of good reasons for believing in life after death for those who have an open mind on the subject. These are not in themselves *proof*, but if the weight of evidence counts for anything, I would suggest that the balance is very strongly in favour of its truth. Consider the following lines of evidence.

THE UNIVERSALITY OF BELIEF IN LIFE AFTER DEATH

It seems that the human race has a built-in instinct for expectation of life beyond the grave. Billy Graham, who majored in anthropology, says he didn't find a race anywhere in the world that did not believe in life after death.[2] Sir James Frazer, one of the great-

---

1. Blackham, *Objections to Humanism*; cited in Koop and Schaeffer, *Whatever Happened*, 79.
2. Heard on a radio broadcast.

est authorities on primitive peoples, mythology and comparative religion, remarks that "among the savage races of mankind . . . life after death is not a matter of speculation and conjecture of hope and fear, it is a practical certainty, which the individual as little dreams of doubting as he doubts the reality of his conscious existence."[3]

Peter Kreeft has written about what he calls the deepest hope of the human heart—the hope of heaven. In *Heaven: The Heart's Deepest Longing*, he says, "From earliest times humanity has hoped for heaven. The earliest artifacts are burial mounds. The dead were always prepared for the great journey."[4] C. S. Lewis expressed a similar thought in *The Problem of Pain*: "There have been times when I think we do not desire heaven; but more often I find myself wondering whether, in our heart of hearts, we have ever desired anything else."[5] The homing instinct of animals such as cats, dogs, and salmon is quite remarkable. Maybe we, too, have a homing instinct—a yearning for heaven, which, though not on the surface, is nevertheless there.

Even in our modern, secular society, every poll that is taken on the subject indicates that a substantial majority believe in some form of life after death. Is this belief merely wishful thinking arising from some evolutionary process that has produced a growing self-consciousness and a belief in our importance as beings at the top of the evolutionary scale? Or could it be that an eternal and loving God has given us this awareness because he longs to enjoy a relationship with us that will last forever? As the writer of Ecclesiastes put it, "He has set eternity in the hearts of men" (3:11).

THE NATURE OF GOD

The Spanish philosopher Miguel de Unamuno once tried out his theory of belief in God but no heaven on a rather simple-minded

---

3. Frazer, *Belief in Immortality*, 468.
4. Kreef, *Heaven: The Heart's Deepest Longing*, introduction.
5. Lewis, *Problem of Pain*, 116.

peasant. The peasant thought for a minute and then replied, "So what is God for?"[6] A pertinent question! If God is the God of love that the Bible says he is, who created us to enjoy a loving relationship with himself, is it logical to assume that he would enable us to enjoy that relationship for a few years and then cast us aside? Particularly when, as William James put it at 70, "I am just getting fit to live."[7] The God I personally came to know as a teenager sixty years ago is a more wonderful God than that!

When Jesus was disputing with the Sadducees of his day, who did not believe in life after death, he made the telling point that God "is not the God of the dead, but of the living" (Mark 12:27). In response to their materialistic attitude to life, he declared, "You are completely wrong! You don't know what the Scriptures teach. And you don't know anything about the power of God" (v. 24 CEV). The love of God, the faithfulness of God and the justice of God demand that there be life after death.

THE WITNESS OF SCIENCE

In the past, a wrong view of science has often been used to buttress the idea of the non-existence of anything that is not "material" or cannot be demonstrated by logical proof. This is "scientism," the giving to science that which its best practitioners do not claim. Modern quantum theory has long demonstrated the false assumption behind such beliefs.

Speaking about life after death, Dr. Von Braun, who was elected president of the National Space Institute in Washington, DC, in 1975, said,

> In our modern world many people seem to feel that science has somehow made such "religious ideas" untimely or old-fashioned.

---

6. Cited by Yancey, "What's a Heaven For?," *Christianity Today*, October 26, 1998.

7. Cited by Simcox, "Gift of Aging," *Christian Century*, December 2, 1987, 1090–92.

The Reasonableness of Life after Death

But I think science has a real surprise for the skeptics. Science, for instance, tells us that nothing in nature, not even the tiniest particle, can disappear without trace.

Think about that for a moment. Once you do, your thoughts about life will never be the same. Science has found that nothing can disappear without trace. Nature does not know extinction. All it knows is transformation!

Now if God applies this fundamental principle to the most minute and insignificant parts of His universe, doesn't it make sense to assume that he applies it also to the masterpiece of His creation—the human soul? I think it does. And everything science has taught me—and continues to teach me—strengthens my belief in the continuity of our spiritual existence after death. Nothing disappears without trace.[8]

Over the last thirty years much study has been done on the subject of near death experiences (NDEs). Modern technology has proved remarkably effective in resuscitating people who, to all intents and purposes, are clinically dead. Hundreds have described their experiences from "the other side." The publication of *On Death and Dying* by Elisabeth Kubler-Ross in 1969 was a landmark in the development of such studies. Her research was continued by Raymond Moody, whose *Life after Life* went on to sell three million copies, while further investigations were embodied in *At the Hour of Death*, by Kaarlis Osis and Erlendur Haraldsson (1977). Contrary to popular opinion, not all reports of NDEs are pleasant ones. Philip J. Swihart of the Midwest Colorado Mental Health Center, in *The Edge of Death* (1978), and Maurice S. Rawlings of the Diagnostic Hospital in Chattanooga, in *Beyond Death's Door* (1978), have recorded experiences that are terrifying and accompanied with a fearful anticipation of judgment. Later works by psychologist Kenneth Ring (*Life at Death*, 1980), and cardiologist Michael Sabom (*Recollections of Death*,1982), helped put the subject squarely on the scientific map. A 1982 Gallup poll found that an estimated eight million people in the United States have had an

---

8. Von Braun, *Science of Mind* magazine, August 1967.

Part 1: Exploring the Territory

NDE. Whatever we are to make of such experiences, they certainly don't point to a cessation of existence at the moment of death.

However, even science today is reluctant to speak of "proof." Scientific theories are based on reasonable assumptions, based on weight of evidence—evidence that can change with further experience. John Fiske, in *The Destiny of Man*, described the materialistic supposition that the life of the soul ends with the life of the body as "perhaps the most colossal instance of baseless assumption known to the history of philosophy."[9] He believed in life beyond the grave "not in the sense which I accept the demonstrable truths of science, but as a supreme act of faith in the reasonableness of God's work."[10]

The Christian view of life after death is not only supported by all the facts that we are presently aware of, taken as a whole, it is also remarkably consistent within itself. David Winter, in his excellent paperback *Hereafter*, writes:

> Unlike many of the speculative ideas, the Christian doctrine of life beyond death meets the main criteria of a sound working hypothesis: it fits the known evidence, it provides a satisfactory answer to the problem posed, and it does it without either internal or external contradiction. Rightly understood it is a magnificently strong consistent 'system.' In preparing this book, for example, I have not at any point been embarrassed by any detail of the Christian doctrine of resurrection, nor have I found any point at which it raised any problems of inconsistency or contradiction.[11]

EVIDENCE FROM NATURE

If there is no life after death, what are we to make of the seemingly countless illustrations that we are confronted with day after day from the world of nature?

9. Fiske, *Destiny of Man*, 110–11.
10. Fiske, *Destiny of Man*, 110.
11. Winter, *Hereafter*, 25.

William Jennings Bryan, in his address *The Prince of Peace,* declared,

> Christ gave us proof of immortality, and yet it would hardly seem necessary that one should rise from the dead to convince us that the grave is not the end. If the Father deigns to touch with divine power the cold and pulseless heart of the buried acorn and to make it burst forth from its prison walls, will He leave neglected in the earth the soul of man, made in the image of his Creator?[12]

Could we have a more wonderful analogy of the reality of resurrection than the transformation of the caterpillar into the butterfly? As Hugh Ross says in *Beyond the Cosmos,* "God has given us sneak previews of our future in new dimensions—in his Word, his Creation, his Incarnation and in his Atonement."[13] Maybe we just need to have our eyes opened to what happens all around us.

THE FACT OF REVELATION

It is said that when Socrates drank the poison hemlock and lay down to die, his friends asked, "Shall we live again?" The dying philosopher could only reply, "I hope so. No man can know." But the opinion that we cannot know is an assumption for which there is no logical foundation. If a God does exist who loves us in the way the Bible says he does, and who longs to have a personal relationship with us, it is most logical that he would want us to know, not only that he exists, but also something of his ultimate purposes for us. And if he is indeed God, then he must be able to make himself known.

It has always been the view of Christianity that God has made himself known in specific ways. He has revealed certain things about himself in the world of nature. "God's eternal power and character cannot be seen. But from the beginning of creation, God has shown what these are like by all he has made. That's why those

---

12. Bryan, *Prince of Peace,* 47–48.
13. Ross, *Beyond the Cosmos,* 115.

Part 1: Exploring the Territory

people don't have any excuse" (Rom 1:20 CEV). More specifically, he has made himself known to certain individuals throughout history, and finally, and most completely, by condescending to become one of us in the person of Jesus Christ. "In the past God spoke to our forefathers through the prophets at many times and in various ways, but in these last days he has spoken to us by his Son, whom he appointed heir of all things, and through whom he made the universe" (Heb 1:1–2).

The record of this revelation, so Christians believe, is given to us in the sixty-six books of the Bible, recorded over a period of over a thousand years. This collection of writings, which has topped the best-seller lists since the invention of the printing press, is open for all who wish to check its contents to see if it has the "ring of truth." It would take another booklet to go into all the reasons why millions believe this collection to be the revealed word of the living God. Suffice it to say that when we come to the New Testament and the teaching of Jesus himself, where the revelation is most complete, life after death becomes one of its major themes.

According to my reckoning, there are about 147 statements by Jesus himself in the four books that tell the story of his life and teaching (Matthew, Mark, Luke and John) in which he implies, or clearly states, that there is life after death. Over half of these come in contexts where the emphasis is on reward or punishment for deeds and attitudes in this life. Eleven of his parables (stories he told to illustrate a point) speak of the division that will take place between those who are rewarded and those who are punished when he judges the world.[14] Is it reasonable to suppose that the

---

14. The Wheat and the Weeds (Matt 13:24–30, 36–43).
The Good Fish and the Bad (Matt 13:47–50).
The Wedding Banquet (Matt 22:1–14).
The Faithful and Unfaithful Servants (Matt 24:45–51).
The Wise and Foolish Virgins (Matt 25:1–13).
The Parable of the Talents (Matt 25:14–30).
The Sheep and the Goats (Matt 25:31–46).
The Shut Door (Luke 13:24–30).
The Great Banquet (Luke 14:15–24).
The Rich Man and Lazarus (Luke 16:19–31).
The Ten Trusted Servants (Luke 19:11–27).

person who has had the greatest influence for good in the history of the human race should have been totally wrong in one of the major planks of his teaching?[15]

One of the reasons Christians believe in life after death is simply *because God has said so*—and done so most plainly.

THE RESURRECTION OF JESUS AND THE FAITH OF BELIEVERS

In the booklet *Did Jesus Really Rise from the Dead?*, I have given the weight of historical evidence that is available to us for believing in the truthfulness of the Gospel accounts of Jesus' resurrection. To this we could add the testimony of the countless stories of those who have devoted their lives to Jesus and who have faced death with a confidence that comes from beyond this world. In part 2 of this booklet I have shared some of my favorites.

OUR INGRAINED SENSE OF JUSTICE

However much our consciences may be deadened by misuse, there is within all of us some sense of right and wrong and a desire for justice. We are quick to condemn acts of injustice done by another, even if we are equally quick to overlook our own faults in this regard! Where does this sense of justice come from? Is it only something that has "evolved" over countless millennia, or could it be that the biblical account of a just God who created us "in his own likeness" (Gen 1:26, 27) makes more sense?

If the latter is true, then we have a problem. When we look around us we see injustices everywhere, and we know that most of them will not be sorted out in this life. If there is no judgment beyond death in which a God who is wholly just, and who knows everything, is going to sort things out, then how can we speak of

---

15. I have given some detail on the influence of Jesus Christ in history in the booklet *Is Jesus Really God?* It can be read on www.christianity.co.nz or www.exploringchristianity.com.

Part 1: Exploring the Territory

justice? It simply does not exist. Nevertheless, if it is true, then it does explain perfectly where our sense of justice comes from and also gives us the motivation to work for it in this world. We know that acts of justice will ultimately be vindicated and injustice condemned.

David Winter makes this point: "If he is all-powerful and good—which is what the word 'God' means to most of us—then it seems to me he *must* act to put things right. Justice on a cosmic scale must be done, and must be seen to be done, or God is not God."[16] I would consider this perhaps the strongest argument of all for life after death and a final judgment.

Having explored some of the issues we are faced with when considering the possibility of life after death, I will spend the rest of the booklet/book explaining the Christian view as it is presented to us in the Bible, particularly the New Testament, which tells of the coming of Jesus and the early preaching of his followers. It is not my intention to go into detail about alternative views such as those of Hinduism, Buddhism, Islam or other religions, but where appropriate I will point out some significant differences.

---

16. Winter, *Hereafter*, 85.

PART 2

The Christian View of Life after Death

4

The Nature of Christian Conversion

To understand the true nature of life after death and its certainty for the believer, it is necessary to understand the nature of Christian conversion. The basic problem of the human race, as outlined in the opening chapters of the Bible, is that we are rebels in God's world. Though created for fellowship and partnership with the living God, our first ancestors chose to go their own sinful ways and live independently from him. One of the consequences of this is that God withdrew his Spirit from men and women and we were left in a condition that the Bible describes as being spiritually "dead," that is, empty of God and spiritual life.[1]

The rest of the Bible is the story of God's activity in history to bring us back to himself, culminating in the life, death and resurrection of Jesus Christ. The heart of this message focuses on the cross where Jesus paid the price of our rebellion. As a result of all he achieved on our behalf by his death and resurrection, the way has been opened for us to return to God and once again enjoy all the blessings that come from living in a relationship with him.

---

1. I have described the process of our rebellion and its full consequences more fully in the booklet *Who Am I? Finding My True Identity as a Human Being and as a Child of God*. It can be read on www.christianity.co.nz or www.exploringchristianity.com.

PART 2: THE CHRISTIAN VIEW OF LIFE AFTER DEATH

Our responsibility in this matter is to acknowledge our sins, turn from them and submit our lives to Jesus Christ. When we do, two wonderful things happen. First we receive forgiveness and are accepted into full fellowship with God, as if we had never sinned in the first place. The second, and equally important part of the process, is that the Third Person in the divine Trinity, God the Holy Spirit, comes to live within our human bodies.[2] This experience is described in the New Testament as being "born of . . . the Spirit" (John 3:5), crossing over "from death to life" (John 5:24), being "made . . . alive with Christ" (Eph 2:5), or being "raised . . . up with Christ" (Eph 2:6). A true believer is spoken of as one who already "has everlasting life" (John 6:47) and already has been "raised with Christ" (Col 1:1).

In other words, a true Christian is one who has received the very presence of God into his being. Death in the Bible is often associated with sin or disobedience to God (e.g., Gen 2:17; Rom 5:12; 6:23). When we accept all that Christ has achieved for us on our behalf, the penalty is removed and in a very real sense we are already on the other side of the grave. It is true that our physical bodies, as we know them now, will go through the process of decay and death. But the real *me*—that thinks, hopes, feels, dreams, makes decisions—my personality, described as "soul" in the Bible, will continue in uninterrupted relationship with the living God, the one who planned my existence in the first place. He brought me into being, sent his Son to die for me when I had drifted from him, restored me to spiritual life and committed himself to me by giving me the Holy Spirit, and has given me an inheritance in his kingdom which "can never perish, spoil or fade" (1 Pet 1:3-4). Christians are not going from the land of the living to the land of the dying. They are going from the land of the dying to the land of the living. Andrew Bonar said, "Preparation for death is almost

---

2. I have explained the Trinity in more detail, how God exists in three persons, Father, Son and Holy Spirit, and how these relate to us in our new experience as Christians, in the booklet *Understanding the Trinity*. It can be read on www.christianity.co.nz or www.exploringchristianity.com.

an imagination. A believer does not prepare for death at all. Christ does it for him. The believer prepares for life."[3]

In this sense, death for a believer is incidental. It is not a full stop but a comma (however distressing it may appear at the time) in the ongoing relationship with God that began when he or she first trusted Christ. As we have seen above, it is no more significant than falling asleep. It is a "departure" on an exciting adventure. This is the word that Paul used when facing execution in Rome (2 Tim 4:6). Paul wrote his letters in Greek and this word was used of seamen casting off moorings and setting sail for the open sea. It was also used for the freeing of a man held captive. His shackles were struck off, the prison doors were opened, and he was free to leave the dark gloom of his dungeon and go out into the glory of God's world. Bishop Moule described it as "that delightful moment when the friendly flood heaves beneath the freed keel, and the prow is set straight and finally towards the shore of home, and the Pilot stands on board, at length 'seen face to face' and lo, as He takes the helm, 'immediately the ship is at the land whither they go.'"[4]

It is from this perspective that George MacDonald could write, "I came from God, and I'm going back to God, and I won't have any gaps of death in the middle of my life."[5] Similarly, in *The Meaning of Salvation*, Michael Green says that in the New Testament, "the life to come is represented to us as continuous with this life. Death has been robbed of its significance, and the two poles in the Christian's existence are his conversion and the coming of Christ."[6]

Christian conversion, therefore, involves receiving the life of God himself into our innermost being through the presence of the Holy Spirit. We are "spiritually alive" in New Testament terms. We are in a totally new relationship with the living God, a relationship which physical death cannot affect. A certain Ebenezer Erskine,

3. Bonar, *Heavenly Springs*, 31.
4. Moule, *Second Epistle to Timothy*, 140.
5. McDonald, *Mary Marston*, chapter 57.
6. Green, *Meaning of Salvation*, 185.

speaking of the hour when he accepted Jesus Christ as his Savior, wrote that it was in the summer of 1708 that he "got his head out of time into eternity." However, it is obvious that when we die our present physical bodies, through which we expressed our lives and personalities in this world, will no longer exist. So let's explore the means by which this life will be expressed beyond the grave.

5

Resurrection, Not Reincarnation

Paul finishes his first letter to the Thessalonians with the prayer, "May your whole spirit, soul and body be kept blameless at the coming of our Lord Jesus Christ" (1 Thess 5:23). The Bible distinguishes between the soul—the real living me that inhabits this body; the spirit—the part of me that distinguishes me from mere animal life and enables me to have a relationship with God, who is spirit (John 4:24); and the body, through which my soul and personality is outwardly expressed. However, each of these parts of my nature is vitally connected and important in making me who I am. We are *people*, not parts. In this respect Christianity differs from dualistic ideas that find expression in Eastern religions such as Hinduism and Buddhism, where the body is regarded as something evil in which we are imprisoned and from which we must eventually escape. In this view, which surfaces in much of New Age teaching, we go through many cycles of reincarnation, returning again and again to new bodies in this world. If we are fortunate, by good works and enlightenment we may eventually escape this bondage to our earthly bodies and be absorbed into Nirvana.

Part 2: The Christian View of Life after Death

It is this transformation of the whole person, body included, in our future existence, which is one of the distinctives of Christianity. Bruce Nicholls puts it as follows:

> Hindus may believe in many avatars, descents of God to earth; they may venerate the cross as an act of self-denial and self-sacrifice, which is a Hindu ideal, but they have no answer to the resurrection of the body. If Jesus is the only way to God, it is because the salvation of the person, body and spirit, is a hope profoundly different from all other religious hope. It gives a new dimension to salvation not found anywhere else. It is true that Muslims hope for the resurrection but as a recovery of the pleasures of this life, and certainly not to be transformed into the glory of the image of the risen Christ.[1]

In Genesis 1 we read seven times that everything God created was good. That includes the human body. This is emphasized in the New Testament. When we put our trust in Jesus and receive the Holy Spirit, then our bodies become the "temple" in which he dwells and through which he longs to express something of his own character. "Surely you know that your body is a temple where the Holy Spirit lives. The Spirit is in you and is a gift from God. You are no longer your own. God paid a great price for you. So use your body to honor God" (1 Cor 6:19–20 CEV).

Apologist Ravi Zacharias, speaking of the New Testament emphasis on "Christ in you, the hope of glory" (Col 1:27), also emphasizes this uniqueness of Christianity:

> There is no other world religion or worldview that talks in those terms. In Islam, Allah is seen as distant and totally transcendent. In Buddhism, there is no god. In the core of Hindu thinking, you are, in effect, made to become god. But in the Christian faith, there is the nearness of God. We do not go to the Temple any more to worship; we take the temple with us. This body is the temple of the living God. There is communion. There is intimacy. We understand that this body is where God

---

1. Nicholls, *Is Jesus the Only Way*, 17.

wishes to make His residence, and we see the sacredness of the human body.[2]

It matters, therefore, how we treat our bodies. It is for this reason that Paul argues for sexual purity. "We are not supposed to do indecent things with our bodies. We are to use them for the Lord who is in charge of our bodies. God will raise us from death by the same power that he used when he raised our Lord to life. Don't you know that your bodies are part of the body of Christ? Is it right for me to join part of the body of Christ to an immoral woman? No, it isn't" (1 Cor 6:13–15 CEV).

Christianity, therefore, speaks not of reincarnation, escape from the body, but of resurrection, the recreation of the body. In 2 Corinthians 5, Paul uses two metaphors for this process: that of leaving a tent (a temporary dwelling) for a new permanent house, and that of putting on a new suit of clothes. It is worth quoting this passage in full:

> Our bodies are like tents that we live in here on earth. But when these tents are destroyed, we know that God will give each of us a place to live.
>
> These homes will not be buildings that someone has made, but they are in heaven and will last forever. While we are here on earth, we sigh because we want to live in that heavenly home. We want to put it on like clothes and not be naked. These tents we now live in are like a heavy burden, and we groan. But we don't do this just because we want to leave these bodies that will die. It is because we want to change them for bodies that will never die. God is the one who makes all this possible. He has given us his Spirit to make us certain that he will do it. So always be cheerful!
>
> As long as we are in these bodies we are away from the Lord. But we live by faith, not by what we see. We should be cheerful, because we would rather leave these bodies and be at home with the Lord. But whether we are at home with the Lord or away from him, we still try our best to please him. After all, Christ will judge each

---

2. Jim Daley, "Conversation with Ravi Zacharias," *Decision*, March 2002.

of us for the good or bad that we do while living in these bodies. (2 Cor 5:1–10 CEV)

It is interesting that in Romans 8, where Paul speaks of our adoption as "sons of God" through receiving the indwelling Spirit (v. 15), he goes on to say that this adoption will one day include "the redemption of our bodies" (v. 23). James Packer sums up the New Testament idea of resurrection in these words: "The raising of the body means the restoring of the person—not just part of me—to active, creative and undying life for God and with God."[3]

This means, of course, that if we mess up this life, we don't get another shot at it in some future existence in this world, as is the view of those who hold to a belief in reincarnation. The Bible is very clear on this. For instance, in discussing the uniqueness and finality of Christ's "once for all" death for our sins, a death that never will, or can, be repeated, the writer of Hebrews compares it to our "once for all" death. "Just as man is destined to die once, and after that face judgment, so Christ was sacrificed once to take away the sins of many people" (Heb 9:27–28).

THE GUARANTEE OF RESURRECTION

In the New Testament it is always the resurrection of Jesus that is presented as the guarantee of the resurrection of the believer. Take for instance this statement of Paul in his first letter to the Thessalonians: "We believe that Jesus died and rose again and so we believe that God will bring with Jesus those who have fallen asleep in him" (1 Thess 4:14). In the booklet *Did Jesus Really Rise from the Dead?*, I have explored the historical evidence for the resurrection of Jesus.[4] Here I would like to focus on the significance and nature of his resurrection.

One of today's leading New Testament scholars, Tom Wright, gave an address "Easter and the Launch of the Church" at a

---

3. Packer, *Great Joy*, 145.

4. This can be read on www.christianity.co.nz or www.exploringchristianity.com.

conference on the future of Anglicanism, in which he spelled out four ways the resurrection of Jesus radically changed the views of the first disciples. These four modifications are evident in the earliest Christian writings, in Paul through to Revelation, in Clement and Ignatius through to Justin, Tertullian and Irenaeus—in other words, in the major theologians of the first two centuries of Christianity.

First, "resurrection" is far more central to early Christianity than it ever was to Judaism. Wright, who is also a good historian, sums up very well the perspective of first-century Judaism on life after death and it is worth quoting him at some length:

> Judaism had a wide spectrum of belief about life beyond death, but increasingly in the Second Temple period the Pharisaic belief in resurrection, based on Daniel 12 and Isaiah 26, and sometimes also on Ezekiel 37, gained ground and became mainstream. The Sadducees and probably others too disputed it, apparently denying all post mortem existence. Many Jews copied the platonic world of hellenism and believed in a disembodied blissful immortality. Resurrection was one point on a spectrum of belief; and it was a revolutionary doctrine. It went with the belief that God would vindicate Israel, would release it from slavery to paganism, would restore it to the pre-eminence it had under David and Solomon. "Resurrection" could function as a metaphor for this restoration, as in Ezekiel; it could also function as a metonym for restoration, with the bodily resurrection of all God's people as one part of the whole package. And belief in the resurrection was grounded, again and again in the literature, on two others: first, the belief in Israel's God as the creator of the world, who would therefore restore his good creation; second, the belief in Israel's God as the God of justice, who would bring justice to the world and would raise the dead so that the righteous could be rewarded and the wicked punished.

But the details of what precisely the resurrection body would be like were never spelled out.⁵

However, when we come to the New Testament, the idea of bodily resurrection is no longer one point on a spectrum of belief. There is no part of the New Testament writings after the resurrection of Jesus had occurred where his death and resurrection are not central to the whole message.

Second, "resurrection" for the first Christians was now a two-stage event: Jesus the Messiah as the firstfruits, then all his people, and perhaps all people, at the end, when he returns. "Christ has indeed been raised from the dead, the firstfruits of those who have fallen asleep" (1 Cor 15:20). The idea that one individual would be raised to life and that this resurrection would be the guarantee of a future resurrection of others is never found in Jewish literature of that time. Yet, it is the very foundation of the first, and all subsequent, Christian writings. As Daniel Reid and Tremper Longman put it in a *Christianity Today* article, "The Resurrection is the first line of a new song that will one day enfold the cosmos."⁶

The idea that Jesus would be raised from the dead prior to the ingathering of the major harvest at the general resurrection when Christ returned was not a new idea to God, though it certainly was for the disciples. It was anticipated by the seven major feasts of the Jewish year,⁷ which God had spelled out to his chosen people when he met with them in the desert at Mount Sinai, after their escape from Egypt twelve hundred years before (Lev 23).

Passover and the *Feast of Firstfruits*. These were held during the first Jewish month Nisan. Passover was a celebration of their deliverance from slavery to the Egyptians, when a lamb was sacrificed and the blood sprinkled on the doorposts of each home.

---

5. Wright, "Easter and the Launch of the Church: An Exposition of Luke 24," Wycliffe Hall, 30 June 2002. Obtained from printout.

6. Reid and Longman, "When God Declares War," *Christianity Today*, October 1996.

7. Seven is the number of completion and fulfillment in the Bible (e.g., the seven creation days of Genesis 1 and 2, and the fifty-four sevens of the book of Revelation).

It appears that Jesus, the Lamb of God (John 1:36; Rev 5:6) who came to deliver us from a far greater slavery, slavery to sin, would have been hanging on the cross when the Passover lambs were being offered in the temple (see John 18:28). Passover was immediately followed by the Feast of Firstfruits, when the first sheaves of the barley harvest were offered in the temple. The barley ripened earlier than other crops. The main harvest was yet in the future. Jesus is the "firstfruits" to rise from the dead (1 Cor 15:20) as he is the one who anticipates and guarantees the greater harvest yet to come.

The *Feast of Weeks* or *Pentecost*. This feast was held seven weeks later at the beginning of the third month Siwan. This marked the beginning of the main harvest. In the New Testament, the giving of the Holy Spirit occurred during this feast (Acts 2). The harvest of proclaiming the gospel message and gathering in the converts began on this day.

For the next four months no feasts were held as everyone was busy gathering the harvest of fruit and crops. We are now living in the period of harvest and it is the prime responsibility of the Christian church to be involved in "bringing in the sheaves" (Matt 9:37–38; John 4:35–37).

The *Feast of Trumpets*, the *Day of Atonement*, and the *Feast of Tabernacles*. These three events all occurred in the seventh month, Tisri, and marked the end of the harvest. The Feast of Trumpets was celebrated on the first day of the month. It is significant that in the New Testament the blowing of the trumpet is three times associated with the return of Christ and the raising of the dead (Matt 24:30–31; 1 Cor 15:51–54; 1 Thess 4:15–17). This will mark the end of the spiritual harvest, gathered in through the preaching of the gospel, and will focus on the harvest that the Lord himself will gather, either for reward or judgment (Matt 13:36–43; Rev 14:14–19).

The Day of Atonement was celebrated on the fourteenth day of the seventh month. On that day the high priest would enter the holy of holies, the innermost court of the temple, and sprinkle the blood of the sacrificial lamb on the atonement cover on the ark of the covenant. The removal of sin from the people was symbolized by the confessing of the sins of the people over a goat and sending it into the wilderness. This ceremony looks forward to the day when all that Christ achieved for us by his sacrificial death will be accomplished, and his people will be raised without sin and enabled to enjoy an unfettered relationship with God and one another. The writer of Hebrews in the New Testament spells out in detail the significance of this day for Christians in chapters nine and ten of his letter.

The Feast of Tabernacles immediately followed the Day of Atonement. During this week the people were expected to live in booths made from the branches of trees in remembrance of God's protection and guidance during their journey through the wilderness. It looks forward to the time when God's people will dwell under his full protection and provision in the new heavens and the new earth (Rev 21 and 22).

All this means, of course, that God had it all planned out from the beginning. He is not taken by surprise! It was the disciples who were slow to catch on. They did very quickly, though, when they were confronted with the risen Christ.

Third, the resurrection involved not just resuscitation, a coming back into a life identical to the present one, but a *transformation*. This would not be a transformation into a non-bodily spirit, but into a new body, with very definite links to the old body, but also with significant differences. This is the common understanding of the New Testament, which I will explore further in the next section.

Fourth, we find in the New Testament (not so much in the early fathers, where other concerns predominated) a quite new metaphorical use of "resurrection," associated with conversion, baptism and holy living (e.g., Rom 6:4-5; Col 3:1-2). We looked at this briefly under the heading "The nature of Christian conversion."

One thing is clear. None of these four new understandings of the meaning of "resurrection" would have occurred *unless the tomb of Jesus had been empty*, and *unless the disciples had personally encountered the risen Christ*, as the records confirm that they did over a period of forty days. One could well argue that there is no greater historical evidence for the resurrection of Jesus than this. It was this event that motivated all their actions from then on and resulted in such rapid growth of the Christian church throughout the Roman Empire as recorded in the New Testament book of Acts. They lived in the shadow of the resurrection and their understanding of the Christian life was conditioned by it.

Another prominent New Testament scholar who has summed up very well the effect that the resurrection of Jesus had on the first disciples is Gordon Fee. In *God's Empowering Presence*, he says,

> It was the resurrection of Christ and the gift of the promised (eschatological) Spirit that completely altered the primitive church's perspective, both about Jesus and about themselves. In place of the totally future eschatology of their Jewish roots, with its hope of a coming Messiah and the resurrection from the dead, the early church recognised that the future had already been set in motion. The resurrection of Christ marked the beginning of the End, the turning of the ages. However, the End had only begun: they still awaited the final event, the (now second) coming of their Messiah Jesus, at which time they too would experience the resurrection/transformation of the body. They lived "between the times"; already the future had begun, not yet had it been consummated. From the New Testament perspective the whole of Christian existence—and theology—has this eschatological "tension" as its basic framework.[8]

Edward Gibbon, historian of the Roman Empire, gave this, the confidence of Christians in eternal life, as one of the main reasons for the rapid spread of Christianity—they were gloriously dogmatic about it. Significant evidence of this comes from the catacombs on the outskirts of Rome, where Christians buried their dead. So far some thirty-five of these have been discovered and the total length of the galleries have been calculated at more than five hundred miles. The earliest burials take us back to just before AD 150, only some eighty to ninety years after Paul was martyred there.

8. Fee, *God's Empowering Presence*, 803.

Part 2: The Christian View of Life after Death

Gradually they fell into disuse after the sack of Rome by the Goths in AD 410. Some seventy thousand graves have been counted in them, but this is a mere fraction of the whole, as only part of them have been explored. Since we know that for at least three hundred years, or ten generations, the entire Christian population of Rome was buried in them, the figure could easily run into millions.

The Christians always refused to speak of the departed brother or sister as having died, but rather as of one summoned or called away, *accersitus ab angelis*—"summoned by angels." Side by side in these catacombs lie the rich and poor, slave and free, awaiting in perfect confidence the promised resurrection. The inscriptions reflect this assurance—"Happiest of women"; "Sopronia . . . happy, always living in God"; "Alive in Christ"; "Here rests in the sleep of peace Mala . . . received into the presence of God." *Spes* ("hope") is one of the words most frequently found in these inscriptions. They speak only of peace and joy in death. Here in the catacombs, for the first time in the pagan world, the power of death was denied. This was in stark contrast to the attitude of the rest of the population. Catallus caught the mood of the majority of first-century Rome when he wrote, "Suns may set and rise again. When once our brief light has set, one unbroken night remains."[9]

This transformation in the attitude to death was beautifully captured by the poet George Herbert:

> Death, thou wast once an uncouth, hideous thing,
>   Nothing but bones, . . .
> But since our saviour's death did put some blood
>   Into thy face,
> Thou art grown fair and full of grace.[10]

It is the death and resurrection of Jesus that guarantees the forgiveness and future resurrection of all who choose to unite with Christ and his cause. If we have accepted him as our Savior and Lord, the rest will follow.

---

9. "Catacombs and Christianity," *Buried History*, May 1963.

10. Herbert, *Poetry Foundation* website, www.poetryfoundation.org/poem/181062.

In this regard, it is significant to note that Paul says that if we have received the Holy Spirit, the "Spirit of sonship" or "adoption," and become God's children, then we are "co-heirs with Christ" (Rom 8:15–17). An heir to an inheritance does not receive it because he has worked for it, but it is a privilege and is given to him on the basis of his relationship with the owner. The New Testament declares that "all things were created by [Christ] and for [Christ]" (Col 1:16). It is by virtue of our relationship with him that we can be assured of sharing fully in the inheritance.

The writer of Hebrews describes this hope in the promises of God regarding our future as "an anchor for the soul, firm and secure." It brings us into the very presence of God "where Jesus, who went before us, has entered on our behalf" (6:19–20). It is an anchor that will stand the strain of the greatest storms.

THE NATURE OF THE RESURRECTION BODY

It is the resurrection of Jesus himself that not only guarantees our resurrection, but also gives us clues as to the nature of our future resurrection body. Harry Blamires, in an article "Heaven and Hell" in *Christianity Today*, imagines what it might be like trying to explain to a caterpillar what it means to be a butterfly. Its risen body will be able to fly like a bird and escape all the limitations imposed by gravity on a creature accustomed to drag its long segment from level to level by a cumbrous array of legs. As for "seeing," the caterpillar's rudimentary apparatus that is sensitive to little more than the distinction between darkness and light will be superseded by the butterfly's truly perceptive eyes. Though a caterpillar may have no awareness that it could exist in any other structural form, it is significant that in an encyclopaedia it is defined in terms of its future as a butterfly. It is the larva of the Lepidoptera (butterflies and moths). Blamires says,

> I cannot help wondering what an angel would find if he looked up "Man" and "Woman" in the *Encyclopaedia Caelestis*: "The name given to the larvae of the saved in their prepupal stage as terrestrial beings. They are

two-legged, two-armed, two-eyed and two-eared (and the most degenerate specimens are said to be two-faced!). They are wingless. They have only a rudimentary sensitivity to reality. They tend to measure everything wholly on the basis of their immature understanding as creatures imprisoned in the space-time continuum.[11]

Though we have only limited imagination to explore our future existence in the kingdom of God, let's use it as we see what the clues are. Paul spells out the most important clue. "Our citizenship is in heaven. And we eagerly await a Savior from there, the Lord Jesus Christ, who, by the power that enables him to bring everything under his control, will transform our lowly bodies so that they will be like his glorious body" (Phil 3:20–21). In choosing to become united with Mary's DNA in her womb and come into this world by natural birth, Jesus had taken upon himself our human nature with all its frailty and limitations.[12] In his resurrection he lifted that humanness to a new level (Heb 2:14–15). "Just as we have borne the likeness of the earthy man [Adam], so shall we bear the likeness of the man from heaven [Christ]" (1 Cor 15:49). If our bodies will one day be like his, what is his like?

What is clear from the New Testament accounts of the resurrection of Jesus, is that his physical body was gone from the tomb and that his transformed body was a *real* body. On his first appearance to the gathered disciples he even showed them his wounds, saying to them, "Why are you so frightened? Why do you doubt? Look at my hands and feet and see who I am! Touch me and find out for yourselves. Ghosts don't have flesh and bones as you see I have" (Luke 24:38–39 CEV). This was the *same* Jesus they had seen nailed on the cross. To put their minds at rest he even ate food before them (vv. 41–43). However, there were some things different about the risen Jesus. He could suddenly appear behind locked doors (John 20:19) and vanish in an instant (Luke 24:30–31).

11. Blamires, "Eternal Weight of Glory," *Christianity Today*, May 27, 1991.
12. I have dealt with the true significance of the birth of Jesus in *The Real Meaning of Christmas: The Virgin Birth and All That*. This can be read on www.christianity.co.nz or www.exploringchristianity.com.

There was something about him that transcended the material limitations of this world.

The most detailed passage in the New Testament on the resurrection is 1 Corinthians 15, where Paul devotes the entire chapter to the subject. He deals with the certainty and importance of Christ's resurrection and its consequence for the believer (vv. 1–33), and then spends the rest of the chapter giving details of our resurrection. He describes four differences between our earthly body and our heavenly body. In using the analogy of the transformation of seed into plant that we observe every day in the natural world, Paul declares, "The body that is sown is perishable, it is raised imperishable; it is sown in dishonor, it is raised in glory; it is sown in weakness, it is raise in power; it is sown a natural body, it is raised a spiritual body" (vv. 42–44).

First, it will be *an imperishable body*. Peter also uses the same Greek word for the environment that the new body will inhabit. "Praise be to the God and father of our Lord Jesus Christ! In his great mercy he has given us new birth into a living hope through the resurrection of Jesus Christ from the dead, and into an inheritance that can *never perish*, spoil or fade—kept in heaven for you, who through faith are shielded by God's power until the coming of the salvation that is ready to be revealed in the last time" (1 Pet 1:3–5, italics mine). An imperishable body for an imperishable inheritance! Distortion, decay, and death will have lost their power.

Second, it will be a *glorious body*. In some way it will express the glory of God. We will be seen to be his handiwork. Paul declares that when Jesus returns he will be glorified *in* his holy people (2 Thess 1:10). In *Mere Christianity*, C. S. Lewis gives the following description of our transformed being: "a dazzling, radiant, immortal creature, pulsating all through with such energy and joy and wisdom and love as we cannot now imagine, a bright stainless mirror that reflects back to God perfectly (though of course, on a smaller scale) His own boundless power and delight and goodness."[13]

---

13. Lewis, *Mere Christianity*, 172.

Third, it will be a *powerful body*. No more failure. No more "I can't do this, I can't do that." We will be enabled to do all that God intends.

Fourth, it will be a *spiritual body*. It is interesting that whereas Luke's Jesus declares that his risen body is "flesh and bones" (Luke 24:39), Paul says that "flesh and *blood* cannot inherit the kingdom of God" (1 Cor 15:50, italics mine). In our present physical existence, every cell in our bodies is dependent on blood for its supply of oxygen. "The life of a creature is in the blood" (Lev 17:11). However, there will be something different about the structure of our resurrection bodies and what it is that gives them life. Tom Wright has a helpful comment about this contrast:

> Luke's Jesus insists that he [Jesus] does have "flesh." What Paul means by "flesh," though, is emphatically different; for him, the word "flesh" indicates variously corruptibility, rebellion, sinfulness and death. For Luke, it just means "physicality." Likewise, Paul's phrase "spiritual body," contrasted with the "natural body," is not as in the RSV [Revised Standard Version] and NRSV, a way of saying "non-physical body" as opposed to "physical body"; the contrast he is making is between a body, a physical substance, *animated* by the normal human life on the one hand and by God's Spirit on the other.[14]

Professor D. M. Mackay of Keele University, who was one of Britain's foremost experts in the communications systems of the human brain, also has an interesting comment on this point in an essay in *Inter-Varsity* (1970):

> It is not as disembodied spirits that God promises us eternal life, but as personalities expressed in a new kind of body—what Paul calls a "spiritual body." Just as a message is still the same message, whether it's spoken in words or flashed in Morse code, so, according to the Bible, we shall be the same persons, whatever the material form in which our personalities may be expressed. Nothing in the scientific picture of man, however complete

---

14. Wright, "Easter and the Launch of the Church: An Exposition of Luke 24," Wycliffe Hall, 30 June 2002.

it may one day become, could effect the truth of this doctrine one way or the other.[15]

Paul finishes off 1 Corinthians 15 with some stirring statements. This resurrection will take place "in a flash, in the twinkling of an eye, at the last trumpet" (v. 52). Not all will die, as some will still be living when Christ returns (v. 51). Most of us will still have to face death, but it has been "swallowed up in victory" (v. 54). When something has been "swallowed up" you don't have to worry about it too much! The sting of death (our sinfulness and the problem of facing judgment) has been removed by Christ's death on our behalf and his resurrection (vv. 55–56). It is instructive that he finishes the chapter with a challenge for *this* life: "Therefore my dear bothers, stand firm. Let nothing move you. Always give yourselves fully to the work of the Lord, because you know that your labor in the Lord is not in vain" (v. 58). Nothing that we do out of gratitude to the Lord for what he has done for us will be wasted. What an incentive!

All this is, of course, development *upwards*. At the resurrection we move to a higher, not a lower plane of existence.

HOPE FOR THE PHYSICALLY AND MENTALLY CHALLENGED

If all we have described is true, then imagine what hope this can bring to those who are confined to bodies that prevent them from living the sort of lives that most of us experience. Beethoven, whose music has brought joy to so many, wrote some of his best works when totally deaf. It is recorded that his last words were, "I shall hear in heaven," though there is some disagreement over this.

Peter Chignell, in his autobiography *Set Free, Now a Prisoner*, tells the story of the death of his brother-in-law, Fraser, at the age of 33. Fraser had Down syndrome and he had swallowed his tongue, blocking his air passage. Peter continues:

---

15. Mackay, *Inter-Varsity* magazine, 1970. Cited by Winter, *Hereafter*, 30.

> My mother-in-law fell weeping uncontrollably beside the bed. I knelt beside her and prayed that the Lord would comfort her. Suddenly she gasped, stopped crying and started laughing. I prayed harder, thinking she had gone out of her mind.
> Afterwards I said to her, "Whatever happened, Mum? You were crying one minute and then you started laughing." She replied, "Peter, didn't you see what I saw and hear what I heard?" I asked her to explain.
> "She said, 'When my heart was breaking with sadness, Fraser's voice said, "Mum, I am not in that old body any more. Look up—I am standing beside you. Jesus has let me come and show you my new body." I looked up and there was Fraser standing beside me, speaking clearly, and no longer having the features of a mongoloid. "Do not grieve, Mum, I am so happy to be out of that old earthly body." Then Fraser vanished.'"

Peter explained that from then on, until her death some years later, she never grieved.[16]

Stuart Townend captures this sense of hope beautifully in the last verse of his great song "How Long?"

> But I know a day is coming
> when the deaf will hear his voice,
> when the blind will see their Saviour,
> and the lame will leap for joy.
> When the widow finds a husband,
> who will always love his bride,
> and the orphan finds a father
> who will never leave her side.[17]

One who has expressed this hope very vividly is Joni Eareckson Tada, who was injured in a diving accident in 1967 that left her a total quadriplegic, paralyzed from the neck down. Since then, through her personal faith and the organization she developed for support of people with disabilities, JAF Ministries (Joni and

---

16. Chignell, *Set Free and Now a Prisoner*, 25–26.
17. From Townend's website. Used by permission. http://www.stuarttownend.co.uk/song/how-long.

Resurrection, Not Reincarnation

Friends), she has brought encouragement and practical help to thousands. In her book *Heaven: Your Real Home* she wrote:

> I can scarcely believe it, I with shriveled, bent fingers, atrophied muscles, gnarled knees, and no feeling from the shoulders down, will one day have a new body, light, bright, and clothed in righteousness—powerful and dazzling. Can you imagine the hope this gives someone spinal cord-injured like me? Or someone who is cerebral palsied, brain-injured, or who has multiple sclerosis? Imagine the hope this gives someone who is manic depressive. No other religion, no other philosophy promises new bodies, hearts and minds. Only in the Gospel of Christ do hurting people find such incredible hope.[18]

It is the physical nature of the resurrection which has inspired Joni. She is excited, she writes, "over how like the Rock of Gibraltar heaven is. We shall touch and taste, rule and reign, move and run, laugh and never have reason to cry."[19] She describes a Christian convention at which the speaker, at the close of the message, asked his audience to kneel for prayer. She watched as they did so. But of course she couldn't do it herself. So she couldn't stop the tears. It was particularly hard for her because, brought up in a Reformed Episcopal Church, she had been accustomed to kneeling for prayer. Then she remembered the resurrection:

> Sitting there, I was reminded that in heaven I will be free to jump, dance, kick and do aerobatics. And although I'm sure Jesus will be delighted to watch me rise on tiptoe, there's something I plan to do that may please him more. If possible, somewhere, sometime before the party gets going, sometime before the guests are called to the banquet table at the Wedding Feast of the Lamb, the first thing I plan to do on resurrection legs is to drop on grateful, glorified knees. I will quietly kneel at the feet of Jesus.[20]

---

18. Tada, *Heaven*, 53.
19. Ibid., 70.
20. Ibid., 51.

6

Between Death and Resurrection

What happens to us between the death of our present bodies and the resurrection of the new? There are those who have taken the word "sleep," used fourteen times for the death of believers in the New Testament, to imply that we have no conscious existence during this period.[1] My own view is that the "sleep" refers to the bodily existence rather than the conscious existence of the soul or personality. Though not a life or death issue, there are at least six passages, which to me strongly imply a continued conscious existence in the presence of Christ, at least for believers.

God allowed Peter, Andrew and John to have a vision of Moses and Elijah, both very much alive, talking with Jesus (Matt 17:3). This picture is reinforced by the fact that Elijah was taken to heaven without going through the process of physical death (2 Kings 2:11) as was Enoch (Gen 5:24). Similarly, Jesus declared that Abraham, Isaac and Jacob were still living as, "He is not God of the dead but of the living" (Matt 22:32).

Jesus said to the dying thief, "Today you will be with me in paradise" (Luke 23:43). Would there have been much point in Jesus declaring the man would be "with him" if he was not going

---

1. Matt 27:52; John 11:11; Acts 7:60; 13:36; 1 Cor 11:30; 15:6, 18, 20, 51; 1 Thess 4:13, 14, 15; 5:10; 2 Pet 3:4.

to be conscious of that glorious fact? As the great evangelist D. L. Moody picturesquely imagined it, he could see the two of them walking arm in arm down the streets of the eternal city!

When facing possible execution in prison, Paul declares that if he had the choice between life and death he would prefer to be "with Christ, which is better by far; but it is more necessary for you that I remain in the body" (Phil 1:23–24). Would it have been "better by far" if he had not been aware of it?

Similarly, Paul declared to the Corinthian believers, "We . . . would prefer to be away from the body and at home with the Lord" (2 Cor 5:8).

The writer of Hebrews speaks of "the spirit of righteous [people] made perfect" (Heb 12:23). There is no mention of the body here and it seems to imply an intermediary state.

The writer of Revelation pictures the martyrs who have been sacrificed on the altar crying out for justice, and then continues, "Then each of those who had been killed was given a white robe and told to rest for a little while. They had to wait until the complete number of the Lord's other servants and followers would be killed" (Rev 6:11). The white robe no doubt symbolizes righteousness, holiness and festivity. Though we need to be careful in building our doctrine on the symbolic pictures of Revelation, and it is important to note that it is the blood, not the martyrs themselves, that cries out for justice (see Gen 4:10), the implication here is very strong for continued conscious existence between death, and resurrection and the final judgment. Dr. Herman Bavinck, in his *Reformed Dogmatics*, commented on this passage: "They have a past which they remember, a present in which they live, and a future which they are approaching."[2]

---

2. Bavinck, *Gereformeerde Dogmatiek*, 709–10.

7

The Nature of Heaven

We have looked at the nature of our resurrected bodies. We will be *real* people, more alive than we are today. Now let us explore the nature of our new environment, heaven itself. The Bible does not spell out in detail the nature of heaven and leaves much to our imagination. However, it gives plenty of clues from which I have culled the following:

HEAVEN IS REAL

We tend to think of heaven as somehow being less real than our present existence. However, the New Testament puts it the other way round. Paul says, "Our light and momentary troubles are achieving for us an eternal glory that far outweighs them all. So we fix our eyes not on what is seen, but on what is unseen. For what is seen is temporary, but what is unseen is eternal" (2 Cor 4:17–18). In comparison to things we experience in this life which are "light" and "momentary," the glory that awaits us is "weighty" and "eternal." In other words, heaven is *more real* than life here. I expect to be more alive than I am now, more aware of who I am as a forgiven and transformed child of God, more aware of my potential. We will be *real* people living in a *real* universe.

The Nature of Heaven

The Bible states four times that God will one day create "a new heaven and a new earth" (Isa 65:17; 66:22; 2 Pet 3:13; Rev 21:1). Note that it includes a new earth. If God created this vast universe, even if he took some billions of years to do it (because he *enjoys* creating), it is going to be no problem for him to create a new universe (or renew this one) in which he will enjoy the company of his created and redeemed people for eternity. In the chapter on "The Church and Creation," in my booklet *God's Vision for His Family*, I have explored the biblical basis for believing in the goodness of God's creation and that this created world will itself be part of God's restored and transformed universe.[1]

Archbishop William Temple, alluding to the three great material truths of Christianity—namely, creation, incarnation (Jesus taking human nature), and resurrection—summed up very well the importance of created matter in his Gifford Lectures *Nature, Man and God*, said,

> It may be safely said that one ground for the hope of Christianity, that it may make good its claim to be the one true faith, lies in the fact that it is the most avowedly materialistic of all the great religions. It affords an expectation that it may be able to control the material, precisely because it does not ignore or deny it, but roundly asserts alike the reality of matter and its subordination. Its own most central saying is: The "Word was made flesh," where the last term was, no doubt, chosen because of its specially materialistic associations. By the very nature of its central doctrine Christianity is committed to a belief in the ultimate significance of the historical process, and in the reality of matter and its place in the divine scheme.[2]

It seems likely that, just as our resurrection bodies will be the same bodies with their identities intact (e.g., Jesus' scars), this new universe will be a regenerated universe, purged of all present

---

1. *God's Vision for His Family, the Church: A Call to the Churches of the New Millennium* can be read on www.christianity.co.nz or www.exploringchristianity.com.

2. Temple, *Nature, Man and God*, Gifford Lectures, lecture 19, "The Sacramental Universe," can be read at http://www.giffordlectures.org.

imperfections, rather than a replacement one. Jesus spoke of it as "the renewal of all things, when the Son of Man sits on his glorious throne" (Matt 19:28). The Greek word translated "renewal" is literally "rebirth" and is used of the spiritual rebirth of people in Titus 3:5. This also seems to be the implication of Paul's statement in Romans 8 that "the creation itself will be liberated from its bondage to decay and brought into the glorious freedom of the children of God" (v. 21). Peter does speak of the destruction of this present universe by fire (2 Pet 3:10–13), but maybe this is part of the cleansing process.

It is interesting that in the wonderful vision, which John has of heaven in the last two chapters of the Bible, he sees the Holy City "coming down out of heaven from God" (Rev 21:2). The *origin* of this home for God's people is in heaven. Its *foundation* is in the new earth where God will live with his people (Rev 21:3; 22:3–4). In a very real sense, heaven and earth will have merged.

The Bible also appears to indicate that all that is best in this world of those things that God and humans have experienced and created, will have its counterpart in heaven. "The glorious treasures of the nations will be brought into the city" (Rev 21:26 CEV). C. S. Lewis provides a useful analogy for describing the relationship between our experiences in this life and the next. Writing to his friend Malcolm, he said, "The hills and valleys of heaven will be to those you now experience not as a copy is to an original, nor as a substitute to the genuine article, but as the flower to the root, or the diamond to the coal."[3]

I have often wondered whether the biblical picture of the wolf living with the lamb, the leopard lying down with the goat, the calf with the lion, and a little child leading them (Isa 11:6–9; 65:25) is to be taken merely as a metaphor of peace among humans, or does it imply something more literal? In his book *The Problem of Pain*, C. S. Lewis has an interesting section where he argues for the presence of animals in heaven, not by virtue of right, but because of their relationship to humans.[4]

---

3. Lewis, *Letters to Malcolm*, 84.
4. Lewis, *Problem of Pain*, 109–14.

The Nature of Heaven

And don't be put off by the symbolism that is used in the Bible to describe heaven. This does not make it any less real. John Buckeridge, former assistant editor of *Alpha* in New Zealand, once said that when he was a child he imagined that everyone would be busy digging up the streets. "After all the preacher said that the streets of heaven were paved with gold—so I figured a jack hammer or pick-axe would be a lot more useful than a harp!" Heaven is no more literally made of gold and precious stones than the promised land of Canaan literally "flowed with milk and honey," but the image being presented is clear enough in both cases. It is sad, however, when adults avoid the issues raised by the biblical teaching on heaven by poking fun at its symbolism. C. S. Lewis has a delightful passage in *Mere Christianity* about this:

> There is no need to be worried by facetious people who try to make the Christian hope of "Heaven" ridiculous by saying they do not want to "spend eternity playing harps." The answer to such people is that if they cannot understand books written for grown-ups, they should not talk about them. All the scriptural imagery (harps, crowns, gold, etc.) is, of course, a merely symbolical attempt to express the inexpressible. Musical instruments are mentioned because for many people (not all) music is the thing known in the present life which most strongly suggests ecstasy and infinity. Crowns are mentioned to suggest the fact that those who are united with God in eternity share His splendour and power and joy. Gold is mentioned to suggest the timelessness of Heaven (gold does not rust) and the preciousness of it. People who take these symbols literally might as well think that when Christ told us to be like doves, He meant that we were to lay eggs.[5]

No doubt the reality will be even more glorious than what is indicated to our limited imagination by the symbols.

At this point it may be helpful to compare the first three chapters of the Bible with the last three. Though the writers employ much symbolism, the significance is obvious.

5. Lewis, *Mere Christianity*, 119.

PART 2: THE CHRISTIAN VIEW OF LIFE AFTER DEATH

Genesis 1–3	Revelation 20–22
Disobedience (3:6)	Service (22:3)
The ground cursed (3:17)	No more curse (22:3)
Relationship with God broken (3:23)	Relationship restored (21:3–4)
Spoiled human relationships (3:16)	Evil and division banished (21:8, 27; 22:2)
Pain and suffering (3:16–19)	No more pain or sorrow (21:4)
Death (3:19)	No more death (21:4)
Satan victorious (3:1–7)	Satan judged (20:10)
The gate shut (3:24)	The gate open (21:25)
The tree of life unobtainable (3:24)	The tree of life for all (22:2)

As Anglican scholar John Stott points out in his excellent book *The Incomparable Christ*, the whole focus of John's description of heaven in the last two chapters of the Bible is on life—the book of life (21:27), the water of life (21:6; 22:1–2, 17) and the tree of life (22:2, 14, 19). He adds, "He uses three distinct metaphors. The first is security in the city of God, the new Jerusalem. The second is access to the tree of life in the Garden of Eden restored. The third is the intimate relationship of bride and bridegroom in marriage. John has a remarkable facility for mixing his metaphors. He jumps abruptly from one to another (the city, the garden and the wedding) without any apparent sense of incongruity."[6]

HEAVEN IS GOD CENTERED

On earth we humans have displaced God from the center of things. In our pride we think we can do things better our way, a process that began in the dawn of history (Gen 3). That is why the world is in a mess! However, in heaven God will be the center and focus of his recreated universe. This is beautifully pictured in Revelation 4 and 5. Chapter 4 pictures God on his throne being worshipped as the creator of all things, while chapter 5 speaks of him as the redeemer of his people. There are four concentric circles around the throne. In the immediate vicinity of the throne are the four living creatures (4:6). These have been variously interpreted as either the highest order of created beings or perhaps representative

---

6. Stott, *Incomparable Christ*, 223.

The Nature of Heaven

of the whole of creation. The faces with the likenesses of lion, ox, man and eagle perhaps signifying majesty, strength, wisdom, and swiftness. Whatever they represent, they focus on the holiness and eternal nature of God.

The second circle consists of the twenty-four elders, representative of God's people of all ages, twelve being the number associated with the people of God (twelve tribes of the Israelites in the Old Testament plus twelve apostles, the foundation members of the church in the New Testament). They all wear crowns and are seated on thrones. The New Testament speaks of a "crown that will last forever" (1 Cor 9:25), a "crown of righteousness" (2 Tim 4:8), "a crown of life" (Jas 1:12; Rev 2:10) and "a crown of glory" (1 Pet 5:4) which await those who are faithful to Christ. Whereas in this life crowns are for winners, and when someone wins others lose, in heaven there are crowns and laurels all around! There is also emphasis on reigning with Christ. "To him who overcomes, I will give the right to sit with me on my throne, just as I overcame and sat down with my Father on his throne" (Rev 3:21). "And they will reign for ever and ever" (Rev 22:5). The elders praise God for his work of creation (4:11) and when Jesus, "a Lamb, looking as if it had been slain" (5:6), appears in heaven, they praise him for his work of redemption. "With your own blood you bought for God people from every tribe, language, nation, and race. You let them become kings and serve God as priests, and they will rule on earth" (5:9–10 CEV).

In the third circle are the millions of angels who praise Jesus, who "is worthy to receive power, riches, wisdom, strength, honor, glory and praise" (5:11–12). The fourth and outer circle is represented by "all beings in heaven and on the earth and under the earth and in the sea" (5:13), in other words, all living creatures, who also join in praising God and Jesus.

Because God is central to the whole picture there will be perfect harmony in the new heavens and earth, in contrast to the picture we have here now, where humans have usurped center stage.

It is significant that Jesus is called the Lamb (in Jewish culture the animal of sacrifice) twenty-seven times in the book of

Revelation. It was his sufferings and death on our behalf. which will give us the right to a place in the kingdom of God. In heaven he will forever carry the outward marks of those sufferings. "Only Jesus has the power to save! His name is the only one in all the world that can save anyone" (Acts 4:12 CEV).

In the picture of heaven described in these two chapters of Revelation there is no mention of the third member of the divine Trinity of Father, Son and Holy Spirit. However, the Holy Spirit does appear at the beginning of the book, represented by the "seven spirits before [God's] throne" (1:4). As most of the symbolism of Revelation is taken from the temple worship of the Old Testament, I expect that what John saw was the seven-branched lamp-stand that stood in the priest's court of the temple. I expect that "the river of the water of life, as clear as crystal, flowing from the throne of God and of the Lamb down the middle of the great street of the city" (22:1) also represents the Holy Spirit. It is he who illuminates our lives with the truth of the gospel, who draws us to Christ, who transforms our lives from within, and whose presence in our lives will always be our link with God the Father and Jesus. He is the giver of life, the one who makes all we have been describing a reality in our experience and through us brings glory to the Father and Jesus.

HEAVEN IS FOR RELATIONSHIPS

As I have explored in some depth in the booklet on the Church, God is a *personal* God who exists within himself in loving relationships between the Father, Son and Holy Spirit. He created us to become members of his forever family and to enjoy those loving relationships with him and one another. Through the transforming work of the Holy Spirit, our self-centeredness and those sins that hinder our relationships here will be removed. We will be "conformed to the likeness of his Son" (Rom 8:29; see also 2 Cor 3:18).

Because we maintain our full individuality we will be able to enjoy those relationships to the full. In this respect Christianity is in complete contrast to the Buddhist and Hindu view of the future

The Nature of Heaven

where Nirvana implies the loss of individual identity. The Shakabuku Kyoten, the "conversion manual" of Soka Gakkai, states, "Life after death merges into the Great Life of the Universe; it cannot be found anywhere." This is the general essence of Buddhism. An individual has no existence and thus death's sorrow is overcome and there is no God to confront me for God and I are one. But in the process we lose out on the possibility of meaningful relationships. This is where all the emphasis is in the Bible. It also contrasts with the Muslim view of heaven where the emphasis is on sensual pleasures rather than those which come from loving relationships with God and others as members of God's forever family.

This emphasis on our personal individuality is implied in Jesus' word to the church in Pergamum: "To him who overcomes... I will also give... a white stone with a new name written on it, known only to him who receives it" (Rev 2:17). C. S. Lewis has a thoughtful comment on this statement:

> What can be more a man's own than this new name, which even in eternity remains a secret between God and him? And what shall we take this secrecy to mean? Surely, that each of the redeemed shall forever know and praise some one aspect of the divine beauty better than any other creature can. Why else were individuals created, but that God, loving all infinitely, should love each differently? And this difference, so far from impairing, floods with meaning the love of all blessed creatures for one another, the communion of the saints. If all experienced God in the same way and returned Him an identical worship, the song of the church triumphant would have no symphony, it would be like an orchestra in which all the instruments played the same note.[7]

In other words, we will each have something different to share with others of our experience of God. This is true unity—a union of distinct individuals who unite in our praise of God. For this we were created. This is very different from the pantheistic view of Eastern religions where everything is God. As Lewis says,

---

7. Lewis, *Problem of Pain*, 119–20.

Part 2: The Christian View of Life after Death

"God created: He caused things other than himself that, being distinct, they might learn to love Him, and achieve union instead of sameness."[8]

I have sometimes been asked, "Will we know each other in heaven?" I have always been surprised that people would raise this question. If he created us for the very purpose of having a people on whom he could shower his love and who could enjoy one another as loving members of his family, would he have forgotten to key in the factor necessary for us to know one another? Anyway the Bible is clear on this point. Moses and Elijah knew one another on the Mount of Transfiguration (Matt 17:3). When Paul is giving encouragement to the Christians at Thessalonica who have lost loved ones, he tells them that when Jesus returns "then those who had faith in Christ before they died will be raised to life. Next, all of us who are still alive will be taken up into the clouds *together with them* to meet the Lord in the sky. From that time on we will all be with the Lord forever. Encourage each other with these words" (1 Thess 4:16–18 CEV, italics mine). Paul expresses his disappointment at not being able to revisit his converts in Thessalonica. But at least he can look forward to meeting them again at Christ's return. "After all, when the Lord Jesus appears, who else but you will give us hope and joy and be like a glorious crown for us?" (1 Thess 2:17–19 CEV). When we have this perspective it will affect many of our goals in this life. Jesus indicated in his parable of the Shrewd Manager that we can start building those relationships for eternity now by the generous use of our material possessions (Luke 16:1–15).

One of the great experiences we can anticipate will be the opportunity to enjoy relationships with people of all ages and all cultures. In this life we are severely limited, both by space and time, in the relationships we can enjoy. H. Russell Bernard, a University of Florida anthropologist, and Peter Killworth, an English physicist, have done a study in which they estimate the number of people that most of us know. Asking 1554 people specific questions about their acquaintances, they concluded that the average person knows 290

8. Ibid., 120.

The Nature of Heaven

people.⁹ In God's forever family, however, we will be able to explore relationships with people of all ages and all cultures.

In John's magnificent vision of heaven, he sees "a great multitude that no one could count, from every nation, tribe, people and language" before God's throne and singing his praises (Rev 7:9-10). How we will cope with the language differences, I don't know, but I am certain that will be no problem!

Apart from space and time barriers, it is our sin and self-centeredness that cause most of our problems concerning relationships in this life. Without those problems we will be able to develop those relationships at the deepest level possible. Here we can only have the closest of relationships with a very few people, the closest of all being within marriage. Even then we are only scratching the surface of really knowing each other. There are no doubt also countless people in the world whose personality and gifts would blend very closely with ours, but that opportunity does not exist. In heaven there will not be those limitations. I believe that this is the reason Jesus says there will be no marriage in heaven, "but they will be like the angels" (Matt 22:30). As Howard Marshall commented, "At the resurrection, *all* relationships will be taken up to such a high level that the exclusiveness of marriage will not be a factor in heaven as it is on earth."[10]

I believe it is because of this emphasis on relationships, which we find throughout the Bible, the New Testament letters in particular, that while the Bible story begins in a garden, it ends in a city.[11] In a garden the emphasis is on the beauty of the environment. In the symbolic language of Revelation, though there is still an emphasis on beauty with the precious stones, the streets of gold, the river of the water of life and the tree of life (Rev 21-22), the fact

---

9. Wikipedia, s.v. "Dunbar's Number," http://en.wikipedia.org/wiki/Dunbar's_number.

10. Cited by Clapp, "What Hollywood Doesn't Know," *Christianity Today*, February 1984.

11. Heaven is also called a "country" (Heb 11:15-16) which speaks of its vastness, a "kingdom" (Matt 25:34) which speaks of God's rule and its orderliness, "paradise" (Luke 23:43) which speaks of its delights, and the "Father's house" (John 14:2) which speaks of its permanence and family relationships.

that it is described as a city changes the emphasis somewhat. We are God's *people* (Rev 21:3). *Our* cities tend to be places of smog, slums and noise. We put up high fences and so hardly know the person next door. However, the new earth will be transformed and sin and injustice will be no more. "God has promised us a new heaven and a new earth, where justice will rule. We are really looking forward to that!" (2 Pet 3:13 CEV).

And, believe it nor not, there will be no churches or denominations in heaven! "I did not see a temple in the city, because the Lord God Almighty and the Lamb are its temple" (Rev 21:22). The joy of unhindered relationships will supersede the need for church buildings and the unhelpful divisions caused by denominations will be no more!

It is because of this certainty of renewed relationships that Paul says we are not to "grieve like the rest of men, who have no hope" (1 Thess 4:13) when we have lost Christian friends. That does not mean it is wrong to grieve at all. Grieving is natural and even Jesus wept at the tomb of Lazarus (John 11:35), but our grieving is mingled with hope.

A moving story is told of an English post-office clerk, whose job it was to handle letters that were inadequately addressed. He was at his desk on Christmas Eve. He was brokenhearted because death had taken his little son. He was given a letter addressed in childlike writing to "Santa Claus, The North Pole." Attached to it was a note from a postman giving the address where he had picked up the letter. The clerk was startled because it was his own address. The writing was that of his daughter. And the letter said, "We're very sad at our house this year. My little brother went to heaven last week. You needn't leave me anything. But if you could give Daddy something that would make him stop crying, I wish you would. I heard him say to Mummy that only eternity can cure him. Could you send him some of that?" The good news is that God is able to send us "some of that." This can soften the blow when we lose our loved ones, as we can have a certain hope of a joyful reunion if we are one in Christ.

The Bible is very clear that we are not to get involved with trying to contact the dead which can open us up to all kinds of deceitful and evil influences (Deut 18:9–13). However, if our loved ones are with Christ and we have a relationship with him, we can rest assured of a common bond that one day will be renewed. Several months after Bishop Handley Moule's wife died in July 1915, he wrote in a letter, "Now she dwells in a better country, very far better, where the Lord shines unveiled as the sun of its sky and of its happy field. My eyes are famished for her, but he who took her is with me and she with him, so we are together still in the nearness of the Spirit."[12]

In *Holy Days and Holidays*, compiled by Edward M. Deems, the story is told of an eminent theologian who said that his first idea of heaven was a great city with walls and spires, and a great many angels, but not one person he knew. Then he lost four of his brothers and a friend, and began to know a little about it. He added, "But it was never until I let one of my own children go up to the skies had I any idea as to what heaven was like. Then the second and the third and the fourth child was taken away from me, and there came a time when I lived more with them and with God than here on the earth."[13]

So the best view of heaven comes to you and to me when we have loved ones in that city of light. We are not put on earth to be remembered! We are put here to prepare for eternity and eternal relationships.

HEAVEN IS A PLACE OF JOY

There is much emphasis on joy in the New Testament. Particularly the inward joy that Jesus gives when we have a good relationship with him. Speaking of that relationship at his last meal with them, and likening it to the relationship that exists between a vine and its branches, where the branch draws all its nutrients

---

12. Moule, *Harriot Mary Moule*, 335.
13. Deems, *Holy Days and Holidays*, 325.

from the rest of the vine, he said to his disciples, "I have told you this so that my joy may be in you and that your joy may be complete" (John 15:1–11). In our present existence there is much to cloud our vision and destroy that joy. In heaven those things will be removed forever. "God himself will be with them and be their God. He will wipe away every tear from their eyes. There will be no more death or mourning or crying or pain, for the old order of things has passed away" (Rev 21:3–4). As Bishop Marcus Loane expressed it, "There will be no room for a permissive society . . . or a wealthy elite, or a down-trodden minority; there will be no place for political intrigue, or public wrangling, or partisan interests, or power struggles." St. Teresa made the statement that, from heaven's perspective, the most miserable earthly life will look like one bad night in an inconvenient hotel![14]

The greatest hindrance to our joy in this life is our own sinful, self-centered natures. However, if our lives are submitted to Jesus, he has the power to "present [us] without fault before his glorious presence . . . with great joy" (Jude 24). What it may be like to be so transformed that we will be without any taint of sin is beautifully expressed by Joni Eareckson Tada in *Heaven: Your Real Home*. She explains that as much as she is looking forward to leaving behind her wheelchair, that will not be the best part of heaven. She has learned to cope with hands and legs that won't do as she commands. But she says, "I am sick and tired of fighting my flesh; that is 'the law of sin at work in my members' [Rom 7:23] that just won't do as I command." However, she continues,

> The day is coming . . . when instead of being a hindrance to the spirit, the body will be the perfect expression of the glorified mind, will and emotions. Right now we wear our souls on the inside. But one day we will be "clothed in righteousness" as we wear our souls on the outside, brilliant and glorious.
>
> I can't wait to be clothed in righteousness, without a trace of sin. True it will be wonderful to stand, stretch,

---

14. Cited in Kreeft, *Making Sense out of Suffering*, 139.

and reach to the sky, but it will be more wonderful to offer praise that is pure.

I won't be crippled by distractions, disabled by insincerity. I won't be handicapped by half-heartedness. My heart will join with others and bubble over with effervescent adoration.

For me, this will be the best part of heaven.[15]

Concerning the question about whether we could ever sin in heaven, I understand the emphasis in Scripture to be that we will be so transformed into the likeness of Christ that sinning would be inconceivable. Though the New Testament makes it clear that Satan will be banished forever from heaven's confines, I find a comment by John Donne useful in this regard: "I shall be so like God, as that the devil himself shall not know me from God, so far as to find any more place to fasten a temptation upon me, than upon God; not to conceive any more hope of my falling from that kingdom, than of God being driven out of it."[16]

The only reminder of suffering in heaven will be the five wounds of Christ. There will be nothing to cloud our vision of Jesus, the source of that joy for, "they will see his face, and his name will be on their foreheads" (Rev 22:4). All sources of spiritual, mental or physical darkness will be banished forever "for here will be no night there" (21:25; 22:5). "The glory of God gives it light, and the Lamb is its lamp" (21:23; 22:5).

It is significant that the New Testament does not speak of us "going to heaven" but rather "departing to be with Christ." Many scriptures point to this meeting with the Lord. Jesus prayed, "Father, I want those you have given me to be with me where I am, and to see my glory" (John 17:24). "Then we shall see face to face" (1 Cor 13:12). "With Christ, which is better by far" (Phil 1:23). "We will see him as he truly is" (1 John 3:2). "They shall see his face" (Rev 22:4). James Packer, in his magnificent book *Knowing God*, adds, "It will be like the day when the sick child is at last able

---

15. Tada, *Heaven*, 41.
16. Donne, *Works*, 534.

Part 2: The Christian View of Life after Death

to leave hospital, and finds father and the whole family waiting outside to greet him—a family occasion, if ever there was one."[17]

It is this meeting with Jesus that will no doubt be our greatest joy. This has been the desire of believers down the ages. As the seventeenth-century Reformed pastor Richard Baxter put it in his poetical version of a covenant with God to which his wife, in a former sickness, "subscribed with a cheerful will":

> My knowledge of that life is small,
> The eye of faith is dim;
> But 'tis enough that Christ knows all,
> And I shall be with him.[18]

The blind hymn-writer Fanny Crosby wrote:

> Through the gates to the city in a robe of spotless white,
> He will lead me where no tears will ever fall;
> In the glad song of ages I shall mingle with delight;
> But I long to meet my Savior first of all.
> I shall know Him, I shall know Him,
> And redeemed by His side I shall stand,
> I shall know Him, I shall know Him,
> By the print of the nails in His hand.[19]

When Evangeline Booth, daughter of General Booth, who founded the Salvation Army, was speaking at Tremont Temple, Boston, during the Chapman-Alexander evangelistic campaign in 1909, she declared:

> I want to see John Howard when the last prisoner shall have been reformed, and Florence Nightingale when the last wound shall have been staunched, and John Huss when the last martyr fire shall have burned out, and William Penn when the last heathen shall have been civilised, and Francis Willard when the last lost girl shall have been won, and your great President Lincoln when the last slave shall have been made free, and my father

17. Packer, *Knowing God*, 198.
18. Baxter, *Poetical Fragments*, 62.
19. For the complete hymn, see http://cyberhymnal.org/htm/m/y/mysavior.htm.

and mother; but most of all I want, and I want all of you, to see Jesus.

John Bunyan died of a chill on 21 August 1688, at the home of a grocer in London. He was fifty-nine years old. One of his dying comments was recorded: "Christ is the desire of nations, the joy of angels, the delight of the Father. What solace then, must the soul be filled with that [has] the possession of him to all eternity."[20]

William Hendricksen, in his very scriptural book *The Bible on the Life Hereafter*, points out that in the famous painting by Goetze *Despised and Rejected of Men*, "all the eyes are turned away from the spear-riven and thorn-crowned Saviour. But in heaven our Lord will be the very centre of interest and attention, for *he* will be all-glorious, and *we* will no longer be self-centred."[21]

And if we should think that the emphasis on adoration we find in the New Testament glimpses of heaven should prove boring, then we need to consider the words of Carol Zaleski in her Ingersoll Lecture on immortality, "Adoration cannot be boring, for one is gazing at the face of the beloved, and the face of the beloved is inexhaustible."[22]

We will not only be *with* Christ, the Bible declares that "we will be *like* him" (John 3:2, italics mine). I take this to mean that we will be like him in his moral purity and love. When Charles Spurgeon was a young preacher, he wrote to the aged Horatius Bonar and asked for his picture. The old man sent it and wrote, "Dear Spurgeon: If you had waited a little, you could have had a better likeness, for soon I shall be like Him."

Fear will have no place in heaven as there will be nothing to be afraid of. In the vision of heaven, which John gives us in Revelation 7, we have a pastoral scene where the emphasis is on living under God's protection. "The one who sits on the throne will spread his tent over them. They will never hunger or thirst again, and they won't be troubled by the sun or any scorching heat. The

20. Bunyan, *Grace Abounding*, in Whiting, *Works*, 50.
21. Hendriksen, *Bible on the Life Hereafter*, 59–60.
22. Zaleski, "In Defence of Immortality," in Post and Binstock, *Fountain of Youth*, 125.

Lamb in the center of the throne will be their shepherd. He will lead them to streams of life-giving water, and God will wipe all tears from their eyes" (vv. 15–17).

The emphasis on joy in heaven is underlined by the manner in which the New Testament repeatedly likens the kingdom of God to a feast, particularly a wedding banquet. The first of the "signs" of God's coming kingdom that John records, the turning of water to wine, symbolizing the new life Jesus came to bring, took place at a wedding feast (John 2:1–11). In several of the stories he told, and in other statements, he likened the kingdom of God to a wedding feast or banquet from which some may either excuse themselves or be excluded.[23] In John's great vision of heaven, he hears the final union of Jesus with all his people described as a wedding feast (Rev 19:9). If there is great joy in heaven over just *one* sinner who repents (Luke 15:7, 10), then how much joy will there be when all the lost who have put their faith in Jesus are finally gathered into his kingdom at his return? In his classic *Divine Comedy*, the Italian poet Dante described how he finally arrived in Paradise and heard the heavenly choir singing praises to the Trinity, saying that it seemed like the laughter of the universe.

And I am sure that much of the joy of heaven will also result from its beauty. The story is told of a little girl who was walking with her father on a starry night. When he asked her what she was thinking, she said, "I was thinking that if the wrong side of heaven is so glorious, what must the right side be?" I wonder if our experience will be something like that of the little girl who lost her sight just after her first birthday. When she was twelve, a surgeon was able to operate and give her back her sight. As she looked around on the day her bandages came off, she said to her mother, "Oh, Mummy, why didn't you tell me it was so beautiful?" "I tried, my darling," said her mother, "but I just didn't have the words."

---

23. The Parable of the Wedding Banquet (Matt 22:1–14).

The Nature of Heaven

HEAVEN IS A PLACE FOR CREATIVITY, GROWTH AND SERVICE

The New Testament has very little to say about the activities of heaven, other than that of praise. However, the Creation story emphasizes that we humans have been designed with certain Godlike qualities (Gen 1:26). That certainly includes our creative gifts. Apart from loving relationships, much of our joy in life comes from creating something beautiful or useful. It is one of the ways we express who we are. Though our gifts are as varied as our personalities, we all have *some* gifts. Our opportunities to develop and use those gifts are often thwarted in this life by many negative influences. Yet God created us the way we are for a purpose. It is inconceivable that we will not be given the opportunity to develop our potential to the full in God's perfect re-creation. Jesus' statements about the faithful servants in two of his stories imply responsible activity in heaven: "You have been faithful with a few things; I will put you in charge of many things"; and, "Because you have been trustworthy in a very small matter, take charge of ten cities" (Matt 25:21; Luke 19:17). Maybe there will be new explorations of God's creation to undertake, and much to create ourselves for the glory of God and the enjoyment of others. I believe Ian McClaren got it right when he wrote, "Heaven is not a Trappist monastery. Neither is it retirement on a pension. No, it is land of continual progress."[24]

C. S. Lewis, in his fantasy *The Last Battle*, expresses this idea of growth and progress beautifully. Speaking of those who had fought the last battle and gone "further up and further in," he finishes the story with these words: "All their lives in this world and all their adventures in Narnia had only been the cover and the title page: now at last they were beginning Chapter One of the great Story which no one on earth had read: which goes on forever: in which every chapter is better than the one before."[25]

The most eloquent passage that I have yet come across expressing this idea of growth in heaven comes from the pen of Ellen

---

24. Cited in Graham, *World Aflame*, 256.
25. Lewis, *Last Battle*, 228.

G. White in her book *The Great Controversy*. I certainly don't believe all that she wrote, but this passage fits well with all I gather from the New Testament:

> There the grandest enterprises may be carried forward, the loftiest aspirations reached, the highest ambitions realized; and still there will arise new heights to surmount, new wonders to admire, new truths to comprehend, fresh objects to call forth the powers of mind and soul and body . . . And the years of eternity, as they roll, will bring richer and still more glorious revelations of God and of Christ. As knowledge is progressive, so will love, reverence, and happiness increase. The more men learn of God, the greater will be their admiration of His character . . . The great controversy is ended. Sin and sinners are no more. The entire universe is clean. One pulse of harmony and gladness beats through the vast creation. From Him who created all, flow life and light and gladness, throughout the realms of illimitable space. From the minutest atom to the greatest world, all things animate and inanimate, in their unshadowed beauty and perfect joy, declare that God is love.[26]

Lest we should find it difficult to conceive of growth in our condition of perfect love and sinlessness, it is good to be reminded that in his youth, Jesus, though perfect man at each stage of his development, "grew in wisdom and stature, and in favor with God and men" (Luke 2:52). However many clues we may gather from the Scriptures, it will surpass all that we could imagine. Paul declares, "No eye has seen, no ear has heard, no mind has conceived what God has prepared for those who love him" (1 Cor 2:9).

One thing that is clearly stated is that heaven will be a place of service to God. "His servants will serve him" (Rev 22:3; see also 7:15). What form of activity this involves is left to our imagination. It is true that the Bible says that those who "die in the Lord" will "rest from their labors" (Rev 14:13). But surely that is rest from the *burdensome* nature of much work in this world, rather than from the work itself. It will certainly not be a servile form of work as it

---

26. White, *Great Controversy*, 677–78.

is accompanied by the words: "They will see his face, and his name will be on their foreheads... And they will reign for ever and ever" (22:4–5).

There is one final point I would like to make before moving on. One of the greatest secrets of the Christian life is recognizing our own failures and limitations in order to learn to depend on God. It is often our own pride and self-confidence that gets in the way of enabling God to do in us and through us those things he longs to do. Acknowledging our moral weakness is a necessary prerequisite to finding God's forgiveness. Recognizing our human emotional and physical limitations is part of the process of learning to depend on God's strength. Jesus summed this principle up in the Sermon on the Mount when he declared, "Blessed are the poor in spirit [those aware of their spiritual needs] for theirs is the kingdom of God" (Matt 5:3). Paul had learned this through many painful experiences. He declared, "I will boast all the more gladly about my weaknesses, so that Christ's power may rest on me. That is why, for Christ's sake, I delight in weaknesses, in insults, in hardships, in persecutions, in difficulties. For when I am weak, then I am strong" (2 Cor 12:9–10).

Death is the ultimate sign and evidence of our moral and human frailty. But it is this that gives God his greatest opportunity. Peter Kreeft, in his very thoughtful book *Making Sense out of Suffering*, has a perceptive passage on this:

> Only when we are dissatisfied, only when we are weak, only when we are failures in ourselves, can God come in. Our failure is our success. Death is the supreme failure, the supreme weakness. And it is also God's supreme opportunity and our supreme success, our entrance into heaven and God's entrance into our deepest selves. Teilhard de Chardin sees this in *The Divine Milieu:* "We can set no limits to the tearing up of roots that is involved on our journey into God . . . There is a further step to take: the one that makes us lose all foothold within ourselves . . . What will be the agent of that definitive transformation? Nothing less than death . . . God must, in some way or other, make room for himself, hollowing

us out and emptying us, if he is finally to penetrate into us. And in order to assimilate us in him, he must break the molecules of our being so as to re-cast and re-model us. The function of death is to provide the necessary entrance into our inmost selves."[27]

---

27. Kreeft, *Making Sense out of Suffering*, 152.

8

Stories of Faith

History has provided us with thousands of stories of God's people down the ages who have faced death with an unshakeable faith and a triumphant spirit. What follows are some stories, among the many, that I have gathered over the years. Though this may seem excessive, they are all stories worth telling and preserving for posterity. Though not *proving* the existence of life after death they certainly give us ample indications of the truth of the gospel. The power of the gospel often shines brightest at such times. More than that, such stories offer us lots of encouragement to so live our lives that when the end of our existence here comes upon us, and in whatever manner it comes, we may also be ready for our homecoming.

Jesus calls us not only to live well, but also to die well. In fact, our death can even be an act of worship, offering up our lives to God in death as we have in life. Paul regarded it as such. In the Old Testament, when a sacrifice was made, a drink offering or libation of oil or wine might be poured over it. This completed the offering. In his letter to the Philippians, Paul says, "Your faith in the Lord and your service are like a sacrifice offered to him. And my own blood may have to be poured out with the sacrifice. If this happens,

Part 2: The Christian View of Life after Death

I will be glad and rejoice with you" (2:17). Esther Popel, in *October Prayer*, wrote:

> Change me, oh God,
> Into a tree in autumn.
> And let my dying
> Be a blaze of glory!¹

When Charles Simeon, the influential vicar of Trinity Church in Cambridge, was dying, someone bathed his eyes and asked if he was relieved. Opening them and looking up to heaven, he said, "Soon they will behold all the glorified saints and angels around the throne of my God and Saviour, who has loved me unto death, and given Himself for me; then I shall see Him whom, having not seen, I love; in whom, though now I see Him not, yet believing I rejoice with joy unspeakable and full of glory" (1 Pet 1:8). Then turning his eyes toward his friend, he added, "Of the reality of this I am as sure as if I were there this moment."

Sometime later, though suffering much, he said, "My principles were not founded on fancies or enthusiasm; there is a reality in them, and I find them sufficient to support me in death."²

The last words of Charles Spurgeon, the great Baptist preacher, were, "Oh, wifie, I have had such a blessed time with my Lord."³

When D. L. Moody, the American evangelist, was dying, his son was at his bedside and heard him say in slow and measured words, "Earth recedes: heaven opens before me." His son's impulse was to arouse him from what he thought was a dream. "No, this is no dream, Will," he said. "It is beautifull . . . If this is death, it is sweet! . . . God is calling me and I must go."

Later he exclaimed, "This is my triumph; this is my coronation day! I have been looking forward to it for years." Then his

---

1. Popel, "October Prayer," http://allpoetry.com/October-Prayer.
2. Moule, *Charles Simeon*, 175.
3. Day, *Shadow of the Broad Brim*, 227.

face lit up, and he said joyfully, "Dwight! Irene! I see the children's faces!" referring to his two grandchildren, whom God had taken home within the past year. Again he said later, "This is my coronation day! It's glorious!"[4]

Frances Havergal, the well-known blind hymn-writer, died on 3 June 1879. When her family could see the end was near, her sister Ellen recited *Jesus I Will Trust Thee*, and Frances "clearly but faintly sang the whole verse, to her own tune *Hermas*. Then she was desperately sick again, and lay back murmuring, "There now it is all over! Blessed rest!"

"And now," wrote Maria, "she looked up steadfastly as if she saw the Lord . . . for ten minutes we watched that almost visible meeting with her King, and her countenance was so glad, as if she were already talking to him. Then she tried to sing, but after one sweet high note, 'He . . .' her voice failed, and she passed away. Our precious sister was gone—satisfied, glorified—within the palace of her King!"[5]

A Boston merchant, Mr. Cobb, declared on his deathbed,

> It is a glorious thing to die. I have been active and busy in the world. I have enjoyed it as much as anyone. God has prospered me. I have property enough, but how small and mean does this world appear on a sick-bed! Nothing can equal my enjoyment in the near view of heaven. My hope in Christ is worth infinitely more than all other things. The blood of Christ—the blood of Christ—none but Christ!
>
> Oh, how thankful I feel that God has provided a way that I, sinful as I am, may look forward with joy to another world, through his dear Son.[6]

---

4. Fitt, *Shorter Life of D. L. Moody*, 119–21.
5. Havergal, *Memorials of Francis Ridley Havergal*, 245.
6. *American Baptist Magazine*, vol. 14 (1834), "Memoir of Mr. Nathaniel Cobb."

Part 2: The Christian View of Life after Death

The converted slave trader, John Newton, who became a beloved minister of the gospel and encouraged Wilberforce in his fight against the slave trade, whispered as he lay dying, "My memory is nearly gone, but I remember two things, that I am a great sinner and that Christ—*is a great Saviour*!"[7]

That irrepressible Cornish Christian Billy Bray came downstairs for the last time on Friday, 22 May 1868. To one of his old friends, who asked a few hours before his death if he had any fear of death, or of being lost, he said, "What! Me fear death! Me lost! Why, my Saviour conquered death. If I were to go down to hell, I would shout 'Glory, glory to my blessed Jesus' until I made the bottomless pit ring again, and the miserable old Satan would say, 'Billy, Billy, this is no place for you: get you back.' Then up to heaven I should go, shouting 'Glory! Glory! Praise the Lord!'"

A little later he said, "Glory!" which was his last word.[8]

Christian missionary Geoffrey Bull was held captive by communists for three years at the time of the Chinese invasion of Tibet. He experienced constant interrogation and threat of execution. Later he wrote, "I pictured in my mind's eye that last morning as I was led out to die. Should I preach, should I pray or should I sing? I decided I would sing. I went over in my mind some of the songs of Zion and then chose this great chorus, determined that by His grace these would be my last words before I saw Him face to face.

> "Some golden daybreak Jesus will come;
> Some golden daybreak, battles all won,
> He'll shout the victory, break through the blue
> Some golden daybreak for me, for you."[9]

A Greek named Aristides, in AD 125, wrote to a friend about the new religion called Christianity: "If any righteous man from

---

7. Pollock, *Amazing Grace*, 182.
8. Bourne, *Billy Bray*, 120–21.
9. Bull, *When Iron Gates Yield*, 187–88.

among the Christians passes from this world, they rejoice and offer thanks to God, and they escort his body with songs and thanksgivings as if he were setting out from one place to another nearby."

"Live in Christ, live in Christ," said the dying Scottish Reformer John Knox, "and you need not fear the death of the flesh."

Those at the bedside of the influential New England preacher Jonathan Edwards, thought he had passed from the realms of consciousness. They began to lament the sad loss to the church, only to be stopped by a memorable final sentence: "Trust in God and you need not fear."

Richard Williams, medical missionary to Patagonia, wrote as he lay huddled up in the hull of his little boat, dying of scurvy and starvation,

> Should anything prevent my ever adding to this, let my beloved ones at home rest assured that I was happy, beyond all expression, the night I wrote these lines, and would not have exchanged situations with any man living. Let them also be assured that my hopes were full and blooming with immortality, that Heaven and Love and Christ, which mean one and the same divine thing, were my soul; that the hope of glory filled my whole heart with joy and gladness; and that to me to live is Christ and to die is gain.[10]

Allen Gardiner was the last of the survivors of the seven missionaries who perished of starvation on Terra del Fuego when their relief ship failed to arrive. His final diary entry read, "Great and marvellous are the loving kindnesses of my gracious God."[11]

Among my favorite stories of those who have faced martyrdom for their faith in Christ are some about the Scottish Covenanters

---

10. MacPherson, *Punctuality of God*.
11. Marsh and Stirling, *Story of Commander Allen Gardiner*, chap. 5.

who were executed between the restoration of Charles II and the accession of William III. I have include several of their stories as typical of saints down the ages who have given their lives for their faith. They are particularly relevant in this twenty-first century, when, according to researcher David Barrett, something like one hundred sixty thousand people are killed annually because of their Christian beliefs. These examples are taken from the book *Fair Sunshine* by Jock Purves.

The day before Donald Cargill was executed in 1681, a friend took a written testimony from him in which he wrote, "This is the most joyful day that ever I saw in my pilgrimage on earth. My joy is now begun which I see shall never be interrupted . . . this day I am to seal with my blood all the truths that ever I preached." At the foot of the scaffold he declared to the multitude that had gathered, "I am no more terrified at death, nor afraid of hell, because of sin, than if I had never sinned; for all my sins are freely pardoned and washed thoroughly away, through the precious blood and intercession of Jesus Christ . . . Be not discouraged at the way of Christ and the cause for which I lay down my life, and step into eternity, where my soul shall be as full of Him as it can desire to be." As he climbed the ladder to the scaffold, he declared, "The Lord knows I go up this ladder with less fear, confusion or perturbation of mind, than ever I entered a pulpit to preach."[12]

As Hugh Mackail climbed the ladder of the scaffold, he called out, "I care no more to go up this ladder, and over it, than if I were going home to my father's house." Rung by rung he called aloud, "Every step is a degree nearer heaven." Sitting at the top of the ladder he took out his pocket Bible, and, after addressing the crowds, he read from the last chapter of it. Standing up, the napkin was put over his face; but, lifting it, he declared:

> Now I begin my intercourse with God, which shall never be broken off. Farewell, father and mother, friends and relations; farewell, the world and all its delights; farewell meat and drink; farewell, sun moon and stars. Welcome, God and Father; welcome, sweet Lord Jesus, the

---

12. Purves, *Fair Sunshine*, 190–91.

Mediator of the new covenant; welcome, blessed Spirit of grace, and God of all consolation; welcome glory; welcome eternal life; welcome death.[13]

Archibald Campbell, ninth earl of Argyle, wrote to his daughter-in-law, Lady Sophia Lindsay, on the day of his execution, "What shall I say in this great day of the Lord, wherein in the midst of a cloud, I have found a fair sunshine? I can wish no more for you, but that the Lord may comfort you, and shine upon you as he does upon me, and give you that same sense of his love in staying in the world, as I have in going out of it."[14]

On the morning of his execution, James Guthrie, when asked how he was, replied, "Very well. This is the day that the Lord has made; let us rejoice and be glad in it." Before the scaffold, Guthrie, who had been offered a bishopric and refused it, declared to the great crowd,

> I take God to record upon my soul, I would not exchange this scaffold with the palace and mitre of the greatest prelate in Britain. Blessed be God who has shown mercy to me such a wretch, and has revealed His Son in me, and made me a minister of the everlasting Gospel . . . Jesus Christ is my Life and my Light, my Righteousness, my strength, and my Salvation and all my desire! O Him, I do with all the strength of my soul commend to you. Bless Him, O my soul, from henceforth even forever. Lord, now let your servant depart in peace for my eyes have seen your salvation."[15]

As James Renwick's mother and young sisters gathered with him in prison for his final meal and a time of worship, he gave thanks in these words: "O Lord, [you have] brought me within two hours of eternity, and this is no matter of terror to me, more than if I were to lie down in a bed of roses . . . O! how can I contain this, to be within two hours of the crown of glory."[16]

13. Ibid., 33–34.
14. Ibid., 6.
15. Ibid., 17–19.
16. Ibid., 117.

Part 2: The Christian View of Life after Death

John Dick wrote to his father during his last hours before his execution: "This [has] been one of the pleasantest nights I have had in my lifetime." Among his last words from the scaffold were: "I am come here this day, and would not change my lot with the greatest in the world. I lay down my life willingly and cheerfully for Christ and His cause, and I heartily forgive all my enemies. I forgive all them who gave me my sentence . . . and I forgive him who is behind me [the executioner] . . . Now blessed be the Lord, here is the sacrifice and free-will offering. Adieu, farewell all friends."[17]

Colonel Rumbold's death was a cruel one, but he died saying that if every one of his grey hairs was a life, he would give them all for the Lord Jesus Christ.[18]

James Boig wrote to his brother the day before his execution: "Now I have no time to enlarge, else I would give you a more particular account of God's goodness and dealing with me; but let this suffice, that I am once fairly on the way, and within view of Immanuel's Land, and in hopes to be received an inhabitant there within the space of twenty-six hours at most . . . I have no more spare time. Grace, mercy and peace be with you. Amen . . . Welcome, cross; welcome, gallows; welcome Christ; welcome, heaven and everlasting happiness."[19]

The merchant John Wodrow wrote to his wife from prison on his dying day, "O, my heart, come and see, I beseech you! I thought that I had known something of my dearest Lord before. But never was it so with me as since I came within the walls of this prison. He is without all comparison! O love, love Him! O taste and see! And that shall solve the question best."[20]

Archibald Alison declared at the scaffold, "What think ye of Heaven and Glory that is at the back of the Cross? The hope of this makes me look upon pale death as a lovely messenger to me. I bless the Lord for my lot this day . . . Friends, give our Lord credit; He is

17. Ibid., 163, 165.
18. Ibid., 185.
19. Ibid., 189–90.
20. Ibid., 28.

aye good, but O! He is good in a day of trial, and He will be sweet company through the ages of Eternity."[21]

Almost the last thing the great preacher F. B. Meyer did, was to send a postcard in a shaky hand to Lindsay Glegg with the words, "I have raced you to heaven. I am just off—see you there. Love, F. B. Meyer."[22]

The story is told that Glegg asked his doctor how much longer he had to live. The doctor replied, "Just a few more hours, say till four o'clock." At this Dr. Meyer went to sleep and woke later in the afternoon. His first question was, "What is the time, nurse?" "Six o'clock," she replied. "Tut, tut," said Meyer, "this will never do. I ought to have gone two hours ago."[23]

Dr. Cicely Saunders, a world authority on the care of the dying and founder of the hospice movement, told of a woman called Louie who had had a grim life. She was born with such brittle bones that she had spent all her life in bed. Far from complaining, her sufferings had only deepened her faith in God. On one occasion, Dr. Saunders, when talking with her about the Christian faith and its relevance to the plight Louie was in, spoke of meeting the Lord at death. "And when it has really happened, what's the first thing that you will say to him?" she asked. Louie's reply was instantaneous, "Oh! I'll say, 'I know you.'"[24]

When the prominent Anglican clergyman David Watson was dying of cancer, he wrote, "The words 'Christ has died, Christ has risen, Christ will come again' should not be mumbled, but shouted with ringing confidence. It's the greatest good news that we could ever know on this earth. Whatever may happen, the best is yet to be."[25]

21. Ibid., 50.
22. Glegg, *Four Score*, 32.
23. Ibid., 32–33.
24. Cited in Green, *Man Alive!*, 81.
25. Watson, *Fear No Evil*.

Part 2: The Christian View of Life after Death

John Paton, pioneer missionary to the New Hebrides, tells in his autobiography how he was challenged by an elderly gentleman who complained that he would be eaten by cannibals:

> At last I replied, "Mr. Dickson, you are advanced in years now, and your own prospect is soon to be laid in the grave, there to be eaten by worms; I confess to you, that if I can but live and die serving and honouring the Lord Jesus, it will make no difference to me whether I am eaten by cannibals or worms; and in the Great Day my resurrection body will arise as fair as yours in the likeness of our risen Redeemer." The old gentleman, raising his hands in a deprecating attitude, left the room exclaiming, "After that I have nothing more to say!"[26]

When the brilliant scientist Michael Faraday was dying, someone asked him, "Sir, what are your speculations now?" He replied, "Speculation? I have none, thank God. I am not resting my dying soul on guess-work, but on the finished work of Christ. 'I know whom I have believed and am persuaded that He is able to keep that which I have committed to Him against that Day' [2 Tim 1:12]."

A Methodist bishop tells how, as a young minister, he was called to the bedside of an elderly woman who was approaching the end of life. He tried to comfort her and muttered something about how sorry he was that she was going to die, when she interrupted him, "God bless you, young man. There's nothing to be scared about. I'm just going to cross over Jordan in a few hours, and my Father owns the land on both sides of the river."

When Joseph Addison lay dying, he sent for his stepson, Lord Warwick, a young man who had lived a rebellious life. When he arrived, Addison said to him, "I have sent for you, son, that you may see in what peace a Christian can die."

---

26. Paton, *Missionary to the New Hebrides*, 56.

Billy Graham told in *Decision* magazine how Dr. W. E. Sangster, England's great Methodist preacher, wrote to him when he was dying of muscular atrophy, "Billy, all my life I have preached that Jesus Christ is adequate for every crisis. I have but a few days to live, and oh, Billy, Christ is indeed adequate in the hour of death. Tell everyone it is true. Tell them for me that God is wonderfully near his children when they come to the end of life's road."[27]

On the morning of his death, the Scottish Covenanter Robert Bruce came down to breakfast with his family. Suddenly he called out, "Hold, daughter, hold. My Master is calling me." He asked for a Bible to be brought and opened at Romans, chapter 8. As his sight was failing, he quoted much of the last part of the chapter till he came to the last two verses, "For I am persuaded that neither death nor life, neither angels nor demons, neither the present nor the future, nor any powers, neither height nor depth, nor anything else in all creation, will be able to separate us from the love of God that is in Christ Jesus our Lord" (Rom 8:38–39). He asked that his finger be placed on those words and said, "God be with you, my children. I have breakfasted with you, and shall sup with my Lord Jesus this night. I die believing these words."[28]

When the saintly H. S. Laird was dying, his young minister son went to his bedside and asked, "Dad, how do you feel about the whole experience?" He turned his face toward his son and replied, "Son, I feel like a little boy on Christmas Eve."

After a bad night, the Russian writer Dostoevsky said to his wife, "I must die today. Light a candle, Anya, and give me the gospel." She handed him a battered New Testament. It had been the only book permitted him during the first three of his four years in a Siberian prison three decades before.

---

27. Graham, in *Decision* magazine, April 1974.
28. As quoted by Fleming, *Fulfilling of Scripture*, 379.

The dying man called his little son, Fyodor, and his daughter, Lyubov, to his side and asked that the parable of the prodigal son be read to them. Anna read the passage from Luke 15, and then Dostoevsky said to them,

> Children, never forget what you have just heard here. Preserve an unbounded faith in the Lord and never despair of his forgiveness. I love you dearly, but my love is nothing in comparison to the Lord's infinite love for all men whom he has created.
>
> If ever it should happen that in the course of your life you commit an offence, you must not lose hope in the Lord. You are his children. Humble yourselves before him, as your Father; beg him for forgiveness, and he will rejoice at your repentance, as he rejoiced at the return of the prodigal son.

That evening he died and his daughter, Aimee, wrote, "I have been present at many deathbeds, but none was so radiant as that of my father. He saw without fear the end approaching. His was a truly Christian death. He was ready to appear before his Eternal Father, hoping that to recompense him for all that he had suffered in this life, God would give him another great work to do, another great task to accomplish."[29]

In his autobiography, *Then Sings My Soul*, American gospel singer George Beverly Shea tells how, when his father fell asleep for the last time, he had a notebook on his lap in which were these words, the last he had written, "Life has been wonderful, the promises of God precious, the eternal hope glorious."[30]

When he knew that he had only a few hours to live, Mr. Gammon, a missionary in southern central Africa, said, "I'll sail in the morning... When I go, set the clock going at Home Sweet Home." (The clock belonged to his colleague's wife and played that tune).[31]

---

29. Boreham, *Prodigal*.
30. Shea, *Then Sings My Soul*, 94.
31. Evans, *Dan Crawford*, 76.

Dr. Leslie Weatherhead wrote about how, in his pastoral ministry, he sat with a dying man who was conscious to the end. "He gripped my hand and I must have gripped his more tightly than I thought I was doing, for he said, 'Don't hold me back. I can see through the gates. It's marvellous.'"

Just before being executed by the Nazis for his faith, Hermann Lange wrote to his parents. The death he had faced for so many months was now imminent. He said, "I am first in a joyous mood. And second filled with great anticipation." His joy came from "faith in Christ who has preceded us in death. In Him I have put my faith and precisely today I have faith in him more firmly than ever." After encouraging them to turn to the New Testament for consolation, he said, "Look where you will, everywhere you will find jubilation over the grace that makes us children of God. What can befall a child of God? Of what should I be afraid? On the contrary, rejoice."[32]

The distinguished German theologian Dietrich Bonhoeffer, also executed just days before the German surrender, shared a service with his fellow prisoners before being taken out to his death, at which he read the text, "Praise be to the God and Father of our Lord Jesus Christ who in his mercy gave us new birth into a living hope by the resurrection of Jesus Christ from the dead" (1 Pet 1:3). As the guards removed him, he sent this last message to the Bishop of Chichester, "This is the end—but for me the beginning of life."[33]

When English cricketer and missionary C. T. Studd died in the heart of Africa, the last word he wrote was, "Hallelujah!" The last word he spoke was "Hallelujah!"[34] The mission sent a message back to London, "Bwana [an honorific title] glorified July 16th."[35]

32. Cited in Green, *Runaway World*, 88.
33. Cited in Green, *Man Alive!*, 84.
34. Grubb, *C. T. Studd*, 242.
35. Grubb, *After C. T. Studd*, 11.

Part 2: The Christian View of Life after Death

Jack Armstrong, a member of the Christian organization Navigators, serving on the *Atlanta* during World War II, wrote in a letter, "What a privilege to give our lives for our country! What a hope a Christian has after death—eternity with the Lord Jesus Christ, and loved ones!" Shortly after, in a post-midnight battle off Guadalcanal, he was fatally wounded. As the chaplain sought to minister to him where he fell, both legs shot off, Jack protested, "Don't bother with me. I know where I'm going," urging the chaplain to spend time with the unsaved.[36]

Sir David Brewster, inventor of the kaleidoscope, said, as he was dying, "I shall see Jesus who created all things . . . I shall see him as he is . . . I have had the light for many years. Oh, how bright it is! I feel so safe and satisfied."[37]

Henry Venn, founder of the Anglican Church Missionary Society, retired from being Vicar of Huddelsfield and went to live in Clapham, next to his son John's rectory, in 1796. When told that he was dying, "the prospect made him so jubilant and high-spirited that his doctor said that it was his joy at dying that kept him alive for another fortnight."[38]

A friend visited Augustus Toplady, author of the popular hymn *Rock of Ages*, just before his death. He felt his pulse and told him that his heart was evidently beating weaker and weaker every day. Toplady replied immediately with the sweetest smile, "Why, that is a good sign to me that death is fast approaching and, blessed be God, I can add that my heart beats every day stronger and stronger for glory."[39]

---

36. Skinner, *Daws*, 218.
37. Gordon, *Home Life of Sir David Brewster*, 410.
38. Hennell, *John Venn and the Clapham Sect*, 151; cited in Stott, *Christ the Liberator*, 37.
39. Ryle, *Christian Leaders*, 370.

Jean Rees tells in *His Name Was Tom*, the biography of her husband, British evangelist Tom Rees, how she was at her father's bedside when he was dying. She said, "A number of us were present, including the nurses and the doctor, when father looked round and said, 'If I should meet my Maker tonight, I will say, "I want no other argument, I need no other plea. It is enough that Jesus died, and that He died for me."'" Those were his last words.[40]

Lady Jane Grey was Queen of England for sixteen days. Because she refused to renounce her simple faith in Christ, she was condemned to be executed. On mounting the scaffold she addressed the spectators, "I die as a true Christian woman, and I look to be saved by no other means but only the mercy of God and the blood of his Son, Jesus Christ." At the close of her address she knelt and repeated the fifty-first psalm. The executioner knelt and asked her forgiveness, which she willingly granted, and said, "I pray you, dispatch me quickly." Tying a handkerchief around her eyes, she felt for the block and laid her head on it with the words, "Lord, into your hands I commend my spirit." She was seventeen years old.[41]

A moving story is told in Graham Twelftree's *Drive the Point Home*. A young man, Jimmy Lee Davis, was sentenced to death row for rape and murder. Even his mother wrote to the state governor, "Don't reprieve him. What he has done is so bad I want my boy to die." A news magazine from America carried the headline "'I Want My Son to Die,' Says Mother." A young Pentecostal man in Melbourne, Australia, read the story. He was moved to write to Jimmy and tell him that Jesus loved him. To his amazement he got a letter back saying, "It's the most wonderful letter I have ever had in my life. I do wish I could meet you. I just wish I could know Jesus in my life like you do. I've made such a mess of it. You have given me hope."

The young man felt that God wanted him to go to America and visit Jimmy. After prayer and sharing the idea with friends,

---

40. Rees, *His Name Was Tom*, 156.
41. Reece, *Compendious Martyrology*, 18–19.

he raised the money and went. By a series of coincidences he got permission to go into death row twice a week, for four hours a visit, for two months. He took his guitar and they sang choruses, told jokes, laughed and he led Jimmy to Jesus. His last visit was to Jimmy's baptism.

For two years Jimmy's faith grew. In one of his letters, he wrote, "There is one thing I'm not going to do. I'm not going to dishonour the gospel by using my conversion to escape the death penalty." Then one day the young man in Melbourne got a ring from his wife, "Can you come home at once? Jimmy's just got permission to ring us from prison; he's being executed tonight." He tore home and got through to the prison two hours before Jimmy was due in the gas chamber. But he just broke down and cried on the phone. However, Jimmy at the other end said, "I love you man. Thank you for all that you have done for me. I've got to go now. Goodbye." And Jimmy hung up.[42]

Colin Chapman, in *The Case for Christianity*, quotes Ugandan bishop Festo Kivengere's account of the 1973 execution by firing squad of three men from his diocese:

> As we walked into the centre of the stadium, I was wondering what to say. How do you give the gospel to doomed men who are probably seething with rage?
>
> We approached them from behind, and as they turned to look at us, what a sight! Their faces were all alight with an unmistakable glow and radiance. Before we could say anything, one of them burst out, "Bishop, thank you for coming! I wanted to tell you. The day I was arrested, in my prison cell, I asked the Lord Jesus to come into my heart. He came in and forgave me all my sins! Heaven is now open, and there is nothing between me and my God! Please tell my wife and children that I am going to be with Jesus. Ask them to accept him into their lives as I did."
>
> The other two men told similar stories, excitedly raising their hands, which rattled with handcuffs.

---

42. Twelftree, *Drive the Point Home*, 119–20.

I felt that what I needed to do was to talk to the soldiers, not to the condemned. So I translated what the men had said into a language the soldiers understood. The military men were standing there with guns cocked and bewilderment on their faces. They were so dumbfounded that they forgot to put the hoods over the men's faces.

The three men faced the firing squad standing close together. They looked towards the people and began to wave, handcuffs and all. The people waved back. Then shots were fired and they were with Jesus . . . It was a day never to be forgotten. Though dead, the men spoke loudly to all of the Kigezi District and beyond, so that there was an upsurge of life in Christ, which challenges death and defeats it.[43]

Karla Faye Tucker was sentenced to death in a Texas prison for murder. During her period in prison she had become a Christian and had a positive ministry to other inmates. In an article about the ministry of the prison chaplain Jim Brazzil in *Christianity Today*, by Virginia Stem Owens, he described how, before her execution, Karla Faye asked to borrow his Bible. He gave it to her while he went to see the warden. When he returned she handed it back without saying anything. Next day, while working on her funeral, he picked up his Bible and flicked it open. There was her message. She had written,

Chaplain/Jim

Thank you for bringing the love & fellowship of Jesus to me as I was preparing to be face to face w/Him. *You*, my precious brother, are hand-picked of God, because of the compassion in your heart, to minister to those who have to walk this road. May the grace and peace of God continue to cover you in a mighty way all of your days!

I love you in Christ
Your Sister, Karla Faye
Ps. 16:11[44]

---

43. Chapman, *Case for Christianity*, 64–65.
44. Owens, *Christianity Today*, May 21, 2001.

Part 2: The Christian View of Life after Death

Rev. Roger Thompson is one of our much-respected Anglican clergymen in Christchurch, New Zealand. His wife, Reena, told me how his grandmother was watching over his grandfather as he was dying. Suddenly he sat up, his face lit up, and he said in an excited voice, "Coming, Jesus." Then he sank back on his pillow and passed on from this life.

9

What about Judgment?

OUR ACCOUNTABILITY TO GOD

According to Morton Kelsey, in his book *Encounter with God*, there are 147 references to judgment in the New Testament.[1] Why should we fight shy of the thought of God as judge? Theologian James Packer says, "Would a God who did not care about the difference between right and wrong be a good and admirable being? Would a God who put no distinction between the beasts of history, the Hitlers and Stalins, and his own saints be morally praiseworthy? . . . The final proof that God is a perfect moral being, not indifferent to questions of right and wrong, is the fact that he has committed himself to judge the world."[2]

It is interesting that one of the sins the Old Testament prophets railed against was the ridicule some people made of the idea God would see and judge their sins.[3]

---

1. Kelsey, *Encounter with God*, 245.
2. Packer, *Knowing God*, 130.
3. E.g., Ps 10:11; Isa 5:18–19; Jer 5:12; Amos 9:10; Mic 2:6–7; Zeph 1:12.

Part 2: The Christian View of Life after Death

If we find the idea of God judging the world difficult to swallow, it may be worth our while to consider the alternative. Pastor Richard Wurmbrand spent fourteen years in a Communist prison, much of it in solitary confinement. In his book *Tortured for Christ*, he says,

> The cruelty of atheism is hard to believe, when man has no faith in the reward of good or the punishment of evil. There is no reason to be human. There is no restraint from the depths of evil, which is in man. The communist torturers often said, "There is no good, no hereafter, no punishment for evil. We can do what we wish." I have heard one torturer say, "I thank God in whom I don't believe that I have lived to this hour when I can express all the evil in my heart." He expressed it in unbelievable brutality and torture inflicted on prisoners.[4]

One thing that is clear from the beginning to the end of the Bible is that God is not only a God of love, compassion and mercy, but also a God of justice, holiness, righteousness and purity. Consequently, we live in a moral universe and are accountable to God as to how we live.[5] It is against the background of moral law, which is the expression of God's own righteous character that we begin to see the necessity of judgment. It was right at the beginning of God's relationship with his people that he gave them a summary of his moral laws in the form of the Ten Commandments (Exod 20:1–17; Deut 5:6–21). Until the people recognized the moral nature of the God they worshipped (in marked contrast to the surrounding pagan gods) and the moral demands he made upon them, they would never recognize their moral failures and need for forgiveness. Nor would the sacrifices he gave them to atone for their sins make any sense. Of course these sacrifices, of themselves, could never take away their sins, but looked forward to the day when Christ would offer that perfect sacrifice which can bring us

---

4. Wurmbrand, *Tortured for Christ*, 34.

5. I have gone into this in some detail in the booklet *Does It Matter How We Live? A Christian View of Morality*, which can be read on www.christianity.co.nz or www.exploringchristianity.com.

perfect forgiveness for all eternity (see Heb 9 and 10). It is in this sense that Paul declares that "the law was put in charge to lead us to Christ" (Gal 3:24).

Without the moral law we would never see our need of Christ. The great American revivalist of the nineteenth century Charles Finney said that the easiest men to win for Christ were lawyers. They understood the inexorable nature of law. There could be no trifling with the demands of law. If the foundations of governments were to be preserved and order maintained, law must be enforced. It was useless to speak of mercy, nor dare the law show mercy. The righteous demands of the law must be met. If the blow does not fall on the wrong-doer, then it must fall on one who makes himself responsible, and accepts the punishment for the wrong entailed.[6]

When the Old Testament speaks of God judging people, either individuals or nations, the emphasis is on his judgments in this present earthly existence. The New Testament also has things to say about God working out his judgments in this life. However, with the added revelation that comes to us in the New Testament, with God breaking into this world in the person of Jesus Christ, the emphasis shifts to a more final and complete judgment that is yet in the future. The guarantee that this will take place, and that goodness and morality will be seen to have won the day in the end, is the resurrection of Jesus Christ from the dead. "God . . . commands all [people] everywhere to repent. For he has set a day when he will judge the world with justice by the man he has appointed. He has given proof of this to all [people] by raising him from the dead" (Acts 17:30–31).

JESUS OUR JUDGE

It is significant that this final great event is referred to clearly or by implication in all twenty-seven books of the New Testament, except for Titus and the brief personal letters of Philemon, 2 John and 3 John. It is often directly associated with the personal return

---

6. Huegel, *Cross through the Scriptures*, 42.

PART 2: THE CHRISTIAN VIEW OF LIFE AFTER DEATH

of Jesus Christ, who is specifically declared to be the one appointed by God the Father to be our judge. "The Father . . . has entrusted all judgment to the Son, that all may honor the Son just as they honor the Father . . . the time is coming when all who are in the graves will hear his voice and come out—those who have done good will rise to live, and those who have done evil will rise to be condemned" (John 5:22, 28-29).[7] John Stott declares, "Thus Jesus Christ, who originated all things as Creator, will consummate all things as Judge. For he is 'the Alpha and the Omega [first and last letters of the Greek alphabet], the First and the Last, the Beginning and the End.' These very same titles are attributed both to God (Rev 1:8) and to Christ (Rev 1:17; 22:13)."[8] There are passages indicating that angels will also have a part to play in the judgment and even humans some role, as Christ's agents.[9]

KEEPING PERSPECTIVE

Although in this final section of this book on life after death we must honestly face all that the New Testament declares about judgment, it is important to keep a right perspective. The emphasis is not first and foremost on judgment but on the amazing grace of God, who has acted in Jesus not only to save us from ultimate condemnation, but to restore us to a vital relationship with himself, a relationship that will last forever. Jesus himself declared that the purpose of his coming into this world was not to judge people but to save them. "God did not send his son into the world to condemn the world, but to save the world through him" (John 3:17). He has made provision for our forgiveness, for reconciliation and for us to grow into all that he originally planned that we should be. And he did this at infinite cost to himself. If we should reject his

---

7. See also Dan 7:13-14; Matt 7:22-23; 13:40-43; 16:27; 25:31-32; 28:18; Acts 10:42; 17:31; Rom 2:16; 2 Cor 5:10; Phil 2:9-10; 2 Thess 1:7-10; 2 Tim 4:1, 8; Jas 5:8-9; Rev 14:14-16.

8. Stott, *Incomparable Christ*, 229.

9. For angels, see for instance, Matt 13:41-42; 24:31; 25:31; 2 Thess 1:7; Rev 14:17-19. For humans, see Ps 149:5-9; Matt 19:28; 1 Cor 6:2-3.

love and refuse his offer, the responsibility for the consequences of that choice will be ours alone.

JUDGMENT AND THE NATURE OF GOD: LOVE AND ANGER

The New Testament makes two unequivocal statements about the nature of God. It declares that "God is light; in him there is no darkness at all" (1 John 1:5) and "God is love" (1 John 4:8). Light and darkness often appear in the New Testament as metaphors of good and evil. It is because God, in his very nature, contains no trace of evil in any form, and because he is love, that we may have perfect confidence in his ability to judge fairly. "Will not the Judge of all the earth do right?" (Gen 18:25). We may be sure, as Paul declares, that "God's judgment is based on truth" and that "God does not show favoritism" (Rom 2:2, 11).

It is important, however, to note the use of the word "anger" or "wrath" in connection with God's attitude toward sin, as this is a reality we must face. The idea that God cannot be angry is neither Hebrew nor Christian, but something borrowed from Greek philosophy. Every novice in Greek philosophy knew that deity must be *apathes*, without disturbing emotions of any kind. As Edwyn Bevan has pointed out, "The idea of the divine anger was not something which penetrated into Christianity from its pagan environment; it was something which the church maintained in the face of adverse pagan criticism."[10]

The idea that God can be angry underlines the fact that he is a *personal* God, which is a distinctive emphasis of Christianity, based on our understanding of the Trinity. In an article in *The New Bible Dictionary*, R. V. G. Tasker writes, "It is inadequate to regard this term [wrath] merely as a description of the 'inevitable process of cause and effect in a moral universe' or as another way of speaking of the results of sin. It is rather a personal quality without

---

10. Bevan, *Symbolism and Belief*, 210.

which God would cease to be fully righteous and His love would degenerate into sentimentality."[11]

Renowned theologian Paul Tillich says, "The idea of the divine wrath has become strange to our time. We have rejected a religion which seemed to make God a furious tyrant, an individual with passions and desires who committed arbitrary acts." But he goes on, "This is not what the wrath of God means. It means the inescapable and unavoidable reaction against every distortion of the law of life, and above all against human pride and arrogance."[12] When rightly understood, it has a certain logical necessity. Stephen Neill wrote some time ago, "His wrath is no more than the clear shining of His light, which must go forth implacably to the destruction of all darkness . . . It is only the doctrine of the wrath of God, of His irreconcilable hostility to all evil, which makes life tolerable in such a world as ours."[13]

Maybe, as R. W. Dale has pointed out, "It is partly because sin does not provoke our own wrath, that we do not believe that sin provokes the wrath of God."[14]

The Old Testament speaks of God's just anger against sin some 580 times, using twenty different words to describe it. This clearly indicates that judgment is more than the working out of the unfortunate consequences of our sin. God is active in judging evil and we stand guilty before him when we break his moral laws. In the New Testament, two words are used, *thumos* and *orge*. They may both be translated by expressions such as "indignation," "anger," "wrath," or "fury." The first is used mainly of human anger, but is used seven times of God's anger in Revelation (14:10, 19; 15:1, 7; 16:1, 19; 19:15). The second word is used of human anger in a few instances, but is used about thirty times of the wrath of God. It is something that may be experienced in this life, but is often associated with the final judgment in phrases such as "the day of God's wrath, when his righteous judgment will be revealed"

---

11. Tasker, "Wrath," in *New Bible Dictionary*, ed. Douglas, 1341.
12. Tillich, *Shaking of the Foundations*, 71.
13. Cited by Carey, *Gate of Glory*, 53.
14. Dale, *Atonement*, 338–39.

(Rom 2:5) or "the great day of their [God's and the Lamb's] wrath has come" (Rev 6:17).

It is important to note the difference between human and divine anger. So often our anger is tainted by selfishness, hurt feelings, and lack of control. As James declares, "Everyone should be quick to listen, slow to speak and slow to become angry, because our anger does not produce the righteousness that God desires" (Jas 1:20). However, God's anger is wholly consistent with his character of holiness and love. It is an action rather than an emotion, his just and consistent attitude toward evil. The Bible declares that "God is love" (1 John 4:8) but it never says that "God is anger." The "anger" of God is the outworking of his character of love as it makes its impact on those who spurn that love. Renowned Swiss theologian Emil Brunner went a step further when he declared, "The wrath of God is the love of God in the form in which the man who has turned away from God and turned against God experiences it."[15]

It is significant also that the Greek words *hilasmos* and *hilasterion* are used several times in the New Testament in connection with what Jesus achieved for us on the cross.[16] They are variously translated by "expiation" or "propitiation." Though scholars debate the exact meaning of these words, there is a strong implication that Jesus took upon himself the full effect of God's "wrath" that our sins deserved. This would be consistent with Paul's statement that "he became a curse in our place" (Gal 3:13).

This was the cup that Jesus requested his Father to take from him, if that was possible (Matt 26:39)—the "cup of . . . wrath" (Isa 51:17; cf. Jer 25:15; Ps 75:8). As there was no other way to gain our salvation, he drank it down to the dregs.

---

15. Brunner, *Man in Revolt*, 187.
16. See 1 John 2:2; 4:10; Rom 3:25.

PART 2: THE CHRISTIAN VIEW OF LIFE AFTER DEATH

THE BASIS ON WHICH JUDGMENT WILL BE MADE

In considering this matter it is important to keep in mind two issues that are clear in the New Testament.

First, the basis on which we are accepted or rejected for a place in God's kingdom will be whether or not we have acknowledged our sins, turned from them, and put our trust in the saving grace of Jesus. *None will be in heaven because they deserve to be there.* The ultimate question will be whether our names are in the "Lamb's book of life" (Rev 13:8; 17:8; 20:12, 15; 21:27). They are those who have repented, put their trust in Jesus as their Savior and Lord, and received the Holy Spirit and the gift of eternal life.

Second, though we can do nothing to earn our salvation—it is a gift to be received by faith—it is interesting that judgment in the New Testament is always on the basis of what we have *done* (or *not* done!).[17] As Klyne Snodgrass says, the Scriptures "consistently teach that judgment is according to works."[18] As John Stott explains, "The reason for this is that the Judgement Day will be a public occasion, and that good works will be the only public and visible evidence which can be produced to attest the authenticity of our faith." As James says, "Faith without works is dead" (2:26).

Of course, this is not to deny that there are those such as the dying thief on the cross (Luke 23:40–43) who have no opportunity to demonstrate the reality of their repentance and faith. If, however, his life had been spared, no doubt this would have been plain for all to see.

Jesus also made it plain that judgment would be on the basis of light received and the opportunities given. In one of his parables, Jesus said that "the servant that knows his master's will and does not get ready or does not do what his master wants" will receive a harsher penalty than the one who "does not know and does things deserving of punishment," for "from everyone who has

---

17. See, for instance, the following passages: Matt 16:27; 25:31–46; John 5:29; Rom 2:5–11; 2 Cor 5:10; Rev 20:13; 22:12.

18. Snodgrass, *Between Two Truths*, 95.

been given much, much more will be demanded; and from the one who has been entrusted with much, much more will be asked" (Luke 12:47, 48). He also indicated that the cities of Korazin and Bethsaida would be worse off in the "day of judgment" than Tyre and Sidon, for if the latter cities had had the opportunity to observe his ministry and miracles "they would have repented long ago in sackcloth and ashes." Similarly, Capernaum would be worse off than the wicked city of Sodom, because if the people of Sodom had had the opportunities that Capernaum was given, their repentance would have spared them the destruction they experienced (Matt 11:20–24).

CHRISTIANS INCLUDED IN THE JUDGMENT

The New Testament is very clear that those who have come to Christ in repentance and faith and accepted him as their Savior and Lord are fully accepted as his sons and daughters. They are freely forgiven and receive the Holy Spirit "who is a deposit guaranteeing our inheritance until the redemption of those who are God's possession—to the praise of his glory" (Eph 1:14). Our standing with God is summed up in the term "justified," used about forty times in the New Testament. It is a legal term emphasizing that we are acquitted of all the charges against us. What Jesus did for us in bearing our sins on the cross and rising again, is sufficient to save us for all eternity. As the writer of Hebrew puts it, "He is able to save completely those who come to God through him, because he always lives to intercede for them" (7:25). The Scriptures are very clear that "there is now no condemnation for those who are in Christ Jesus" (Rom 8:1).

However, this does not mean that true believers will not face judgment as to what we have done with what we have been given. Paul underlines the fact that "we must *all* appear before the judgment seat of Christ" (2 Cor 5:10, italics mine). In 1 Corinthians 3 he likens our lives to a building. The only solid foundation on which we can build our lives is our relationship with Jesus Christ. However, having laid this foundation, we can then go on to build

Part 2: The Christian View of Life after Death

with materials that will stand the test of time and eternity, or those that will, in the end, prove worthless. "Whatever we build on that foundation will be tested by fire on the day of judgment. Then everyone will find out if we have used gold, silver, and precious stones, or wood, hay, and straw. We will be rewarded if our building is left standing. But if it is destroyed by fire, we will lose everything. Yet we ourselves will be saved, like someone escaping from flames" (vv. 12–15 CEV).

God knows the motivations of our hearts. It is not our apparent success or failure that he is ultimately concerned with but whether our sincere desire has been to please him and do his will. In the following chapter Paul has more to say on this point. He has been receiving criticism from some regarding his work and ministry. His response is one we would all do well to take note of: "Since our first duty is to be faithful to the one we work for, it doesn't matter to me if I am judged by you or even by a court of law. In fact, I don't judge myself. I don't know of anything against me, but that doesn't prove that I am right. The Lord is my judge. So don't judge anyone until the Lord comes. He will show what is hidden in the dark and what is in everyone's heart. Then God will be the one who praises each of us" (1 Cor 4:2–5 CEV).

Just what will be the nature of the rewards and punishments believers will receive we can safely leave in his loving hands. I love the attitude of a certain Brother Paul, a Franciscan friar, in this respect. He wrote,

> In September I had my 74th birthday. It has been a very happy life. It has been fulfilling and rewarding ... But the last few years I have begun to realise that this journey is a pilgrimage and I long for the journey's end. When I was a boy away at school, it seemed the Christmas holidays would never come so I could join old friends and my loving family. And, oh, the excitement and joy of the trip back home!
>
> It seems to me that death is like going home for Christmas. God is our all-wise and everlasting Father and to die is to return home to His love. He is love, his love is a free unearnable gift and given for all time. It is

WHAT ABOUT JUDGMENT?

true, of course, that he is also Judge but he is Judge and my Wise and Loving Father. I can trust his Judgment as I trust his love. And this I know; he loves me!

In January I had an emergency prostate operation. It was cancerous and the cancer has spread apparently to my whole bone structure and to one kidney. Where else it may be I do not know, and frankly, I don't care.

I am delighted because I can see not-too-far-ahead that journey's end for which I have waited. My bags are all packed and Christmas is coming! Whatever time God calls me, I will be going home for Christmas. It will be a Merry Christmas. Rejoice with me—and pray! I love you.

Affectionately, Paul, S.S.F.

Jurgen Moltmann has observed that the phrase "Day of the Lord" in the Old Testament inspired fear; but in the New Testament it inspires confidence, because the authors had come to know the Lord whose Day it was.[19]

I shall let John have the last word: "God is love. If we keep on loving others, we will stay one in our hearts with God, and he will stay one with us. If we truly love others and live as Christ did in this world, we won't be worried about the day of judgment. A real love for others will chase those worries away. The thought of being punished is what makes us afraid. It shows that we have not really learned to love" (1 John 4:16–18 CEV).

A SYMBOL OF MERCY

"God is the only comfort," said C. S. Lewis. "He is also the Supreme Terror; the thing we most need and the thing we most want to hide from. He is our only possible Ally and we have made ourselves His enemy. Some people talk as if meeting the gaze of 'Absolute Goodness' would be fun. They need to think again."[20] However, to encourage us to come to him in repentance and hope, rather than

---

19. Cited in Yancey, *Jesus I Never Knew*, 253.
20. Lewis, *Mere Christianity*, 37.

to run and hide, he has given a lasting symbol of his mercy—the rainbow.

Whether we think of the story of Noah's flood as a worldwide catastrophe, or a local event of universal significance, there are some obvious lessons for us. It is against the background of this judgment that God appears to Noah and makes him a promise that never again will all life be destroyed by a flood of such magnitude. As a pledge that he will keep his word, he says, "I have set my rainbow in the clouds, and it will be the sign of the covenant between . . . me and you and all living creatures of every kind" (Gen 9:13–15).

It is significant that it is always against the background of the storm cloud that the rainbow appears. The diffraction of the light through the raindrops, producing the various colors of the rainbow, is the evidence that somewhere the sun is still shining. In the awesome picture of God's throne that John gives us in the final book of the Bible, Revelation: "a rainbow, resembling an emerald, encircled the throne" (4:3). God's exalted throne is also the throne of grace and mercy. The Bible speaks of God as "slow to anger"[21] and "patient."[22] If we would meet with God as "Ally" rather than as "Terror," then the two requirements necessary are first that we acknowledge sincerely and openly our need of that mercy, and then that we cast ourselves upon it as it is offered us through Jesus. Having done so, then we may "approach the throne of grace with confidence" (Heb 4:16).

---

21. Exod 34:6; Num 14:18; Neh 9:17; Ps 86:15; 103:8; 145:8; Joel 2:13; Jonah 4:2.

22. 1 Pet 3:20; 2 Pet 3:9.

10

The Future of Unbelievers

SOME BACKGROUND TO THE DISCUSSION

Here we come to a subject that is unpopular in today's modern world. Our unease with the subject is demonstrated by that fact that we either joke about it or avoid it altogether. However, to be faithful to the teaching of Jesus, and those he himself taught and commissioned to teach in his name, we cannot avoid it without giving a false picture of the nature of reality.

I am among those who believe the Bible is God's inspired revelation of himself to us humans. The Holy Spirit, working through chosen persons, and using their own individual gifts and perceptions, gave us truth that can be relied on. Though the Bible is our final authority, indeed our only authority on matters such as this that are beyond our experience, it is up to us to attempt to interpret accurately what is written there. We do well to do so with much prayer and humility, recognizing our own limitations of understanding, and proneness to conditioning and prejudice. After all, God does know a little more than we do, and he does not always choose to reveal everything. "The secret things belong to the Lord our God, but the things revealed belong to us and to our children forever, that we may follow all the words of this law" (Deut 29:29). The purpose of Scripture is to bring us into an obedient relationship with himself, not to give us material for idle speculation.

Those who have confidence in the Bible as the authoritative revelation of the living God have tended to hold three views concerning the future of those who have rejected Christ's offer of salvation in this life. Since the time of Origen, a third-century Alexandrian Bible teacher and theologian, there have been people who, while taking seriously the New Testament teaching about the judgment of those who reject the Savior in this life, also believe that opportunity will be given for repentance and salvation in the next life and that eventually all will be included in God's eternal family. In fact, some would say that some of the emphases of Scripture demands it. This is generally known as "universalism." It has been a minority view and I do not have the space to deal with it here, but for those who wish to explore it further I would commend a thoughtful book by Randy Klassen, *What Does the Bible Really Say About Hell?* It is up-to-date, easy to read and has received positive comments from those who may not necessarily hold that view.

The traditional view, held by most of the church fathers, the medieval theologians, the Reformers, and probably most Evangelical leaders today, is that those who have refused Christ in this life will be condemned to eternal separation from God in continued conscious torment. It is not that Christians *want* to believe this (though the way some have preached it, one may be forgiven for thinking that, at least in some cases, this may be the case!). It is just that there seems no other way to interpret some of the passages dealing with the subject in the New Testament.

There is certainly much in the New Testament concerning the suffering of those who reject Christ's offer of forgiveness and reconciliation in this life. I will look at the terms used for this a little further on. The argument that this suffering is *forever* is based largely on the repeated use of the word "eternal" in connection with the fate of the unrepentant, particularly its use in Matthew 25:46, where "eternal punishment" is contrasted with "eternal life."

The Future of Unbelievers

There is also the statement in Revelation 14:11 that "the smoke of their torment rises up for ever and ever."

There is a third view which has been raised as a possible interpretation of relevant New Testament passages which has been variously spoken of as "conditional immortality" or "annihilationism." There is a slight difference between the two. According to the former, nobody survives death except those to whom God gives life. The Scripture declares that God "alone is immortal" (1 Tim 6:16). We, however, are offered immortality through the gospel (2 Tim 1:10). Or, as Paul puts it, if we have accepted Christ, what is mortal will be "clothed . . . with immortality" (1 Cor 15:54). It is something we are given by grace and is not ours by nature. In this view, though the unrepentant may or may not survive death, eventually they will cease to exist because God has not given them eternal life.

The view of annihilationism is that everybody survives death and will eventually be resurrected, but the unrepentant will finally be destroyed. With either conditional immortality or annihilationism, those without Christ will not suffer forever. They will cease to exist. This is a view that has been put forward as a legitimate interpretation of the New Testament evidence by respected biblical scholars such as Alan Bernstein, John Stott, Michael Green, Frank Guillebaud, Clark Pinnock, Edward Fudge, Philip Hughes, William Crockett, Steven Travis, and John Wenham.

INTERPRETING THE BIBLICAL EVIDENCE

Because this third view is the one that people are least familiar with, and because it is one that I believe can legitimately be argued from Scripture, I will explore this in some detail. In his book *Essentials*, which he coauthored with David Edwards, John Stott summarizes the arguments, which tend to support the third of these three options.[1] Stott, one of the most influential Christian leaders of the last generation, is not only a top New Testament scholar,

---

1. Edwards and Stott, *Essentials*, 312–20.

but is also a remarkably clear and logical thinker. The views that I give here are dealt with more fully in his book and I commend it as a good, concise starting point for those who wish to explore the matter further.

First, there is the question of the use of language and the meaning of the terms used. Frequent terminology used in relation to the final state of the lost is that relating to "destruction." The commonest Greek words used are the verb *apollumi* ("to destroy") and the noun *apoleia* ("destruction"). When the verb is active and transitive it means "to kill." It is used in this sense when Herod wanted to kill the baby Jesus and when the Jewish leaders plotted to have him executed (Matt 2:13; 12:14; 27:20). It is used at least twenty-two times in this plain sense. Jesus used this word when he talked of God destroying "both soul and body in hell" (Matt 10:28; cf. Jas 4:12). Stott comments, "If to kill is to deprive the body of life, hell would seem to be the deprivation of both physical and spiritual life, that is, an extinction of being."[2]

When this verb is used in the middle and intransitive tense, then it means to be destroyed and so to perish. It is used often of perishing physically (e.g., Luke 15:17; 1 Cor 10:9), but also, in about nine instances, of those who perish spiritually. Unbelievers are spoken of as "those who are perishing" (1 Cor 1:18; 2 Cor 2:15; 4:3; 2 Thess 2:10). The word used in 1 Thessalonians 5:3 and 2 Thessalonians 1:9 is *olethros*, which also means "ruin" or "destruction." John Stott comments on the use of these terms: "It would seem strange, therefore, if people who are said to suffer destruction are in fact not destroyed; and . . . it is difficult to imagine a perpetually inconclusive process of perishing. It cannot, I think, be replied that it is impossible to destroy human beings because they are immortal, for the immortality—and therefore indestructibility—of the soul is a Greek not a biblical concept."[3]

Some would be more dogmatic than this. R. F. Weymouth, who translated the New Testament into English (first published in 1903) directly from the Greek, after many years of intensive study

---

2. Ibid., 315.
3. Ibid., 316.

The Future of Unbelievers

of textual criticism, wrote, "My mind fails to conceive a grosser misinterpretation of language than when the five or six strongest words which the Greek tongue possesses, signifying 'destroy,' or 'destruction,' are explained to mean maintaining an everlasting but wretched existence. To translate black as white is nothing to this."[4]

Another matter for debate is the meaning and use of the word "eternal," which keeps popping up in the context of both the future destiny of both the saved and the lost. As regards its use at the end of the parable of the Sheep and the Goats where "eternal punishment" is contrasted with "eternal life" (Matt 25:46), Stott comments, "What Jesus said is that both the life and the punishment would be eternal, but he did not in that passage define the nature of either. Because he elsewhere spoke of eternal life as a conscious enjoyment of God (John 17:3), it does not follow that eternal punishment must be a conscious experience of pain at the hand of God. On the contrary, although declaring both to be eternal, Jesus is *contrasting* the two destinies: the more unlike they are, the better."[5]

The issue at stake is whether the word "eternal" refers to the *length* of the punishment, or merely to the *irreversible nature* of the punishment, whatever that punishment might include. There is nothing here that might necessarily preclude the second option.

The second area of debate concerns the *symbolic imagery* used in Scripture to characterize hell, particularly that of fire. The most common expression that Jesus used of hell was *gehenna*, a transliteration from the Hebrew *ge hinnom*. It occurs eleven times in the gospels.[6] Hinnom was a valley south of Jerusalem where, under the kings Ahaz and Manasseh, children were sacrificed in the fire to the god Molech (2 Kgs 16:3; 21:6; 2 Chron 28:3; 33:6). The prophets borrowed the term as a symbol of judgment (Jer

---

4. Cited in White, *Life in Christ*, 365. It is only fair to note, however, that the verb *apollumi* can be used in the sense of "to be spoiled" or "diverted from proper function," as in Mark 2:22 (See also Rom 14:15; 1 Cor 8:11). The noun *apòleia* is also used in the sense of "waste" in Matt 26:8.

5. Edwards and Stott, *Essentials*, 317.

6. Matt 5:22, 29–30; 10:28; 18:9; 23:15, 33; Mark 9:43, 45, 47; Luke 12:5.

7:31–32; 19:6). In Jesus' day, the valley was used as a burial place for criminals and for burning garbage. Closely associated with this imagery is the concept of fire, which is mentioned about twenty times in connection with the final judgment. We read such terms as "hell fire" (literally: "gehenna of fire"—Matt 5:22), "everlasting fire" (Matt 18:8), the place "where the fire never goes out" (Mark 9:43), and "the lake of fire" (Rev 20:15). God himself, in a passage that speaks of final judgment, is spoken of as "a consuming fire" (Heb 12:29). We may well accept that the "fire" is to be taken figuratively and not literally, as is the term "outer darkness" which is used on several occasions.[7] (Anyway, fire and darkness would appear to exclude each other if taken literally.) However, the images that are used are meant to *mean something*.

Stott aptly comments,

> It is doubtless because we have all had experience of the acute pain of being burned, that fire is associated in our minds with "conscious torment." But the main function of fire is not to cause pain, but to secure destruction, as all the world's incinerators bear witness. Hence the biblical expression "a consuming fire" and John the Baptist's picture of the Judge burning up the chaff with unquenchable fire (Matt 3:12; cf. Luke 3:17). The fire itself is termed "eternal" and "unquenchable," but it would be very odd if what is thrown into it proves indestructible. Our expectation would be the opposite: it would be consumed forever, not tormented forever. Hence it is the smoke (evidence that fire has done its work) which "rises for ever and ever" (Rev 14:11; cf. 19:3).[8]

There are other passages where fire is mentioned that are much debated, such as the torment experienced by the rich man in the parable of the Rich Man and Lazarus (Luke 16:19–31), and the statement that some will be tormented "in the presence of the holy angels and of the Lamb . . . And the smoke of their torment rises for ever and ever" (Rev 14:10–11). We must be careful

---

7. Matt 8:12; 22:13; 25:30 (cf. 2 Pet 2:17; Jude 13).
8. Edwards and Stott, *Essentials*, 316.

The Future of Unbelievers

in interpreting a parable, which the story in Luke appears to be, rather than a real-life instance. However, Stott's comment also seems appropriate here:

> These two states were experienced immediately after Dives [the rich man] died (verses 22, 23). The natural interpretation would be that Jesus was referring to the so-called "intermediate (or interim) state" between death and resurrection. I myself believe that this will be a time (if indeed we shall be aware of the passage of time) when the lost will come to the unimaginably painful realisation of their fate. This is not incompatible, however, with their final annihilation. Similarly, the "torment" of Revelation 14:10, because it will be experienced "in the presence of the holy angels and of the Lamb," seems to refer to the moment of judgement, not to the eternal state. It is not the torment itself but its "smoke" (symbol of the completed burning) which will be "for ever and ever."[9]

It is also significant that the statement that the smoke rises "for ever and ever" seems to be an echo of almost identical words in Isaiah 34:10 where the prophet foretells God's judgment on Edom. In Isaiah, these words are immediately followed by the statement that, "none shall pass through it for ever and ever." In other words, it will be completely devoid of human life.

A third word, the use of which is much debated, is the word "all" when it is used in passages that look forward to Christ's universal reign. Jesus said that he would "draw all [people] to himself" (John 12:32). The time is coming when God will "bring all things in heaven and earth together under one head, even Christ" (Eph 1:10). Similarly, "at the name of Jesus everyone will bow down, those in heaven, on earth, and under the earth. And to the glory of God the Father everyone will openly agree, 'Jesus Christ is Lord!'" (Phil 2:10–11). In the end, God will be "all in all" (NIV) or "mean everything to everyone" (1 Cor 15:28 CEV).[10] These verses are often used as an argument for universalism, the belief that all will

---

9. Edwards and Stott, *Essentials*, 317–18.
10. See also Rom 5:18; 11:32; 14:11; 1 Cor 15:22; 2 Cor 5:19; Col 1:20.

Part 2: The Christian View of Life after Death

eventually find salvation and be accepted into God's family. If we are unable to accept this view, on the basis of the repeated warnings of Jesus that judgment will involve a separation into two opposite and eternal destinies, then how do we interpret these passages? Again, Stott comments, "These texts . . . lead me to ask how God can in any meaningful sense be called 'everything to everybody' while an unspecified number of people still continue in rebellion against him and under his judgement. It would be easier to hold together the awful reality of hell and the universal reign of God if hell means destruction and the impenitent are no more."[11]

A third area of debate concerns the biblical vision of justice. Justice, which has its roots in the eternal nature of God, is a major theme of both the Old and New Testaments. It is one of the strongest arguments supporting the idea of a final judgment. One of the songs resounding in heaven when this final event does take place will be, "Salvation and glory and power belong to our God, for true and just are his judgments" (Rev 19:1–2). The New Testament also indicates clearly that the penalties inflicted will be commensurate with the evil done. This being the case, would it be compatible with divine justice to punish for all eternity sins consciously committed in time, however serious those sins might be? There are questions here that only God can answer, and one day we will no doubt know those answers. However, at least from the human perspective, annihilation would seem a more just decision than eternal conscious torment.

I think it is appropriate to give the final statement on this issue also to John Stott. In a personal statement, which he prepared in reply to a number of correspondents who questioned him on these issues, and which Timothy Dudley-Smith records in the second volume of his magnificent biography of Stott's life, he says,

> There is no "knockdown" argument on either side, which effectively settles this issue; both sides are faced with difficult texts. I am disturbed by the excessive dogmatism of those who claim that only one view is biblical. I plead for greater humility of judgment. We evangelical people

11. Edwards and Stott, *Essentials*, 319.

need to give one another liberty in areas in which Scripture is not absolutely plain. F. F. Bruce wrote to me in 1989, that "annihilation is certainly an acceptable interpretation of the relevant New Testament passages." He added, "For myself, I remain agnostic." My position is similar.[12]

SEPARATION AND THE SHUT DOOR

There are two things that are very clear from the New Testament. First, that there are but two possible destinies, either with God or without him. There is no middle ground. A brief skim through the teaching of Jesus in the four Gospels (Matthew, Mark, Luke and John) will confirm this, quite apart from the rest of the New Testament. There is nothing there that would lend weight to any other view.

Following the sinking of the *Titanic*, the White Star office in Liverpool, England, placed a large board on either side of the main entrance. On one they printed in large letters, "Known to Be Saved," and on the other, "Known to Be Lost." When the *Titanic*'s voyage began there were three classes of passengers, but when it ended the number was reduced to only two—those who were saved by the rescue boats and those who were lost in the deep waters.[13] Similarly, when our eternal destiny is at stake, I don't see how you can interpret the New Testament passages on the subject in any other way.

God longs that all should accept his offer of reconciliation, purchased at infinite cost through the atoning death of Jesus. "He is patient with you, not wanting anyone to perish, but everyone to come to repentance" (2 Pet 3:9). However, in his loving purposes he has given us the freedom to choose. Those who choose not

---

12. Dudley-Smith, *John Stott*, 354. The conclusion of personal statement prepared in reply to a number of correspondents who asked him about this question.

13. Adams, *Titanic's Last Hero*, 23.

PART 2: THE CHRISTIAN VIEW OF LIFE AFTER DEATH

to recognize their need and submit to him, of necessity exclude themselves from all he longs to give us.

It will be a most awful thing to hear those words, recorded in the Sermon on the Mount, "I never knew you. Away from me, you evildoers" (Matt 7:23; cf. Luke 13:27). One of the clearest passages, emphasizing this separation from the presence of God, is in 2 Thessalonians: "He will punish those who do not know God and do not obey the gospel of our Lord Jesus. They will be punished with everlasting destruction and shut out from the presence of the Lord and from the majesty of his power on the day he comes to be glorified in his holy people and to be marveled at among all those who have believed" (2 Thess 1:8–10). It is significant the number of times the idea of being "outside" keeps cropping up.[14]

Sadly, those who by choice exclude themselves from God's presence also exclude themselves from the presence of his family. As I have mentioned earlier, God is a God who exists in community of loving relationships, and his whole purpose in creating this universe was to enlarge that community. As mentioned above, one of the terms Jesus used to emphasize the horror of being outside that community is "outer darkness." Whereas the imagery of fire points to destruction, that of darkness speaks of the loss of all relationships, loneliness, separation, alienation and moral blindness. To be separated from God is to be separated from the One who is the ultimate source of all goodness and truth.

The second point is the finality of the sentence. It is hard to avoid the full effect of the word "eternal" when applied to the future of the unrepentant, as well as to the future of those who are welcomed into God's kingdom. It does appear to refer to the final *consequences* of that choice, even if not necessarily to one's continual existence. Though scholars debate the prime significance of its meaning, it seems to include the thought of "irreversible." James Barr says in his book *Biblical Words for Time*, "The cases of *aionios* ["eternal"] refer fairly uniformly to the being of God or to

---

14. Matt 8:12; 22:13; 25:11–12; Luke 13:28; Rev 22:15.

The Future of Unbelievers

plans and realities which, once established by him, are perpetual or unchanging."[15]

Of particular significance in this regard is Jesus' description of "blasphemy against the Holy Spirit" as an "eternal sin" (Mark 3:29). In a similar passage in Matthew's gospel, Jesus enlarges on what is meant by an "eternal sin": "Anyone who speaks against the Holy Spirit will not be forgiven, either in this age or in the age to come" (Matt 12:32). It is the Holy Spirit who seeks to show us our need of forgiveness and who points us to Christ as the answer to that need. My understanding of this "sin against the Holy Spirit" is that we so resist his efforts to impress us with the truth that we become immune to his pleadings to submit our lives to Christ. The religious leaders that Jesus was speaking to on this occasion were in danger of doing this as they were attributing his sheer goodness to the work of Satan.

It is pertinent to ask if Jesus would have said, as he did of Judas, "that man would be better off if he had never been born" (Matt 26:24), if ultimately Judas was to end up in heaven? It is also significant that the writer of Hebrews lists "eternal judgment" as one of the "elementary teachings about Christ" (6:1–2).

Imagery that Jesus used which would strongly support this is that of the "shut door." In the parable of the Wise and Foolish Virgins, those who were unprepared for the bridegroom's return turn up for the celebrations and find the door shut. "'Sir! Sir,!' they said. 'Open the door for us!' But he replied, 'I tell you the truth, I don't know you.' Therefore keep watch, because you do not know the day or the hour" (Matt 25:11–13). On one occasion he was asked the question, "Lord, are only a few people going to be saved?" He refrained from giving a direct answer, but his reply is worth noting in full:

> Make every effort to enter through the narrow door, because many, I tell you, will try to enter and will not be able to. Once the owner of the house gets up and closes the door, you will stand outside knocking and pleading, "Sir, open the door for us." But he will answer, "I don't know you or where you come from." Then you

---

15. Barr, *Biblical Words for Time*, 77.

will say, "We ate and drank with you, and you taught in our streets." But he will reply, "I don't know you or where you come from. Away from me, all you evildoers!" There will be weeping there, and gnashing of teeth, when you see Abraham, Isaac and Jacob and all the prophets in the kingdom of God, but you yourselves thrown out. People will come from east and west and north and south, and will take their places at the feast in the kingdom of God. Indeed there are those who are last who will be first, and the first who will be last. (Luke 13:23-30)

WHAT ABOUT THOSE WHO HAVE NOT HEARD THE GOSPEL?

One question I have not answered yet is, "What about those people who have never heard the gospel, or even the very name of Jesus?" It is estimated that 67 percent of all humans from AD 30 to the present day have never heard of his name. Will they suffer condemnation along with those who have consciously rejected him? This issue also has relevance for those who lived before Christ came, for those who have heard the gospel but only in a manner that distorts its true meaning, for those mentally handicapped persons who lack the ability to understand it, and for children who have yet to reach the age of knowing right from wrong.

It is important to avoid dogmatism on questions that God has not made clear, and this is certainly one of them. However, there are certain principles that are relevant to the discussion about which the Bible is not in doubt.

First, we all stand guilty in the light of God's blazing holiness and purity. Whether we are "big sinners" or "little sinners" is of little account. None of us will get to heaven because we *deserve* to be there.[16] We are wholly dependent on the grace and mercy of God.

16. I deal with this more fully in the booklets *Does It Matter How We Live? A Christian View of Morality* and *Who Am I? Finding My True Identity as a Human Being and as a Child of God*. These can be read on www.christianity.co.nz or www.exploringchristianity.com. On this point, see also Luke 23:34; Acts 3:17; 1 Tim 1:13.

The Future of Unbelievers

Second, when Jesus died on the cross he was taking upon himself the consequences for the sins of the whole human race. "He is the atoning sacrifice for our sins, and not only for ours but also for the sins of the whole world" (1 John 2:2). "God was reconciling the world to himself in Christ, not counting [people's] sins against them" (2 Cor 5:19).

Third, if those who have not heard or understood the gospel make it to heaven, it will not be because they deserved it, but because of the amazing love and saving work of Jesus Christ—whether they heard of it or not. He is "the Savior of the world" (John 4:42; 1 John 4:14). "Only Jesus has the power to save! His name is the only one in all the world that can save anyone" (Acts 4:12). "There is only one God and one mediator between God and people, the man Christ Jesus, who gave himself as a ransom for all [people]" (1 Tim 2:5-6). Jesus himself declared, "No one knows the Father except the Son and those to whom the Son chooses to reveal him" (Matt 11:27), and again, "No one comes to the Father except through me" (John 14:6).

Fourth, God has made it plain, as we have seen above, that he will judge us all fairly on the light we have received and the opportunities we have been given. In his condemnation of the towns of Korazin, Bethsaida and Capernaum, he made it plain that they would be worse off than Tyre, Sidon and Sodom on the day of judgment, as he knew that if the latter cities had seen what they had seen and heard what they had heard, they would have repented.[17]

Apart from these four truths I am content to leave all such matters in God's very capable hands. I am certain that when the final decisions are made we will stand amazed at the wisdom, the justice, the love and the mercy of our God. It is significant that in the story Jesus told of the Pharisee and the tax collector, it was the despised tax collector, who "beat his breast and said, 'God, have mercy on me, a sinner,'" who "went home justified before God" rather than the Pharisee who thought he was a better man and was unaware of his need for forgiveness (Luke 18:9-14). It seems as if

---

17. On this point, see also Luke 23:34; Acts 3:17; 1 Tim 1:13.

Part 2: The Christian View of Life after Death

the Old Testament believers were accepted on the basis of their faith, even though they knew little if anything about the coming of Christ. Norman Anderson writes in *Christianity and World Religions*, "The believing Jew was accepted and blessed not because of the prescribed animal sacrifices he offered, nor even his repentance and abandonment of himself to God's mercy, but because of what God himself was going to do in his only Son at the cross of Calvary."[18]

Though we have all been given the freedom to make moral choices and to choose our attitude to God, I have a conviction that there will be more in heaven than not there. This seems to me to be the implications of Paul's argument in the last half of Romans 5, where he goes to some lengths to show how the grace of God given us in Jesus is greater than the effect of Adam's sin. Though the New Testament indicates that we can be certain of our own salvation and our relationship with God,[19] I am sure there will be surprises when we find who is in heaven and who is not there. This is implied in the statement of Jesus that "there are those who are last who will be first, and the first who will be last" (Luke 13:30). One humorist has written the following little poem:

> I dreamt death came the other night
> And heaven's gate swung wide.
> With kindly grace an angel came
> And ushered me inside:
> And there to my astonishment
> Stood folk I'd known on earth,
> Some I had judged as quite unfit
> Or but of little worth:
> Indignant words rose to my lips
> But never were set free,
> For every face showed stunned surprise
> *No one expected me!*

---

18. Anderson, *Christianity and World Religions*, 153.

19. I deal with this question in the booklet *Can I Know for Sure That I Am Going to Heaven?* This can be read on www.christianity.co.nz or www.exploringchristianity.com.

THE FUTURE OF UNBELIEVERS

—Len Dean[20]

We must constantly remind ourselves of the fact that judging is God's business and not ours. "Judge nothing before the appointed time; wait till the Lord comes. He will bring to light what is hidden in darkness and will expose the motives of [people's] hearts" (1 Cor 4:5; cf. Matt 7:1).

As far as young children are concerned, I take comfort from God's word to his people in the wilderness, when he warned that many of them, because of their rebellion, would not enter the promised land. "The little ones that you said would be taken captive, your children who do not yet know good from bad—they will enter the land. I will give it to them and they will take possession of it" (Deut 1:39).

In the meantime, it is given to us who have found salvation in Jesus Christ, to share the glorious news of what Jesus has done for us, and what he is offering to men and women in this life and the next. "He has committed to us the message of reconciliation" (2 Cor 5:19). No doubt, part of our own judgment will lie in how obedient we have been in discharging this responsibility.

AN APPROPRIATE RESPONSE

If all we have said about judgment is true, and the imagery used points to something that is *real*, then there can be no place for either flippancy or triumphalism as we look out from our secure position in Christ on a world that experiences great need and often a deep longing for answers. John Stott says, "It is not dogmatism that is unbecoming in speaking about the fact of hell; it is glibness and frivolity. How can we even think about hell without tears."[21] Jeremiah, who was called to warn his people of the judgment God would surely bring upon them because of their rebellion against him, declared, "Oh, that my head were a spring of water and my eyes a fountain of tears! I would weep day and night for the slain of

---

20. Source unknown. Said to have been found in an old King James Bible.
21. Stott, *Christian Mission*, 113.

my people" (Jer 9:1; cf. 13:17; 14:17). Jesus wept over the impenitent city of Jerusalem and cried out, "If you, even you, had only known on this day what would bring you peace . . . !" (Luke 19:41–42; cf. Matt 23:37–38). As Paul contemplated his own people who were either rejecting the gospel or ignorant of it, he wrote, "I have great sorrow and unceasing anguish in my heart. For I could wish that I myself were cursed and cut off from Christ for the sake of my brothers, those of my own race, the people of Israel" (Rom 9:3).

One of the most effective evangelists in history, Dwight L. Moody, reportedly said that if we preach on hell, we should do so with tears in our eyes. Though he would occasionally state his belief in the wrath of God and the existence of hell, it was more typical of him to say:

> A great many people say I don't preach the terrors of religion. I don't want to—don't want to scare men into the kingdom of God. I don't believe in preaching that way . . . If I wanted to scare men into heaven, I would just hold the terrors of hell over their heads and say, "Go right in." But that is not the way to win men. They don't have any slaves in Heaven they are all sons, and they must accept salvation voluntarily.[22]
>
> If I could only make people believe God loves them, what a rush we would see for the Kingdom of God.[23]

---

22. Moody, *Gospel Awakening*, 285.
23. Moody, "Love of God," in *Finding God*.

11

A Choice to Be Made

Gladys Hunt, in *Don't Be Afraid to Die*, has this to say: "We are limited by concepts of time and space; we need an eternal point of view. Your reaction to death will be conditioned by your reaction to God. Those afraid of God are most fearful of death. They who know Him well seem to welcome the opportunity of being with Him. That's the dimension that transforms death—knowing God."[1]

If all we have said is true, then sorting out our relationship with God becomes the most important issue we face in this life, not only for our true enjoyment and usefulness in this life, but also for that which lies beyond the grave. And the sooner the better! Blaise Pascal astutely warned in *Pensées*, "Between heaven and hell is only this life, which is the most fragile thing in the world."[2] Longfellow once said, "It is not until time, with reckless hand, has torn half the leaves from the book of human life, to light the fires of human passion with, that [we] begin to see that the leaves which remain are few in number."[3]

---

1. Hunt, *Christian Way of Death*, 102.
2. Cited by Grouthuis "To Heaven and Back," in *Christianity Today*, April 3, 1995.
3. Longfellow, *Hyperion*, book 4, chapter 8.

PART 2: THE CHRISTIAN VIEW OF LIFE AFTER DEATH

God has taken the risk of giving us the freedom to choose which way we will go. We can choose to go all the way with him, or we can silence his voice and face the future on our own. F. W. Robertson described this as God's "terrible permission."[4] G. K. Chesterton once remarked, "Hell is God's great compliment to the reality of human freedom and the dignity of human personality."[5]

And if we wish to sort out our relationship with God we cannot ignore the person of Jesus. Religion can offer you a decent burial. Christ offers you new, abundant and everlasting life. He is the one who came into this world to share our humanity and to pay the penalty for our sins. He has overcome death on our behalf. It is he to whom we must give account on the day of judgment. Anglican scholar and pastor Michael Green gives the following helpful illustration:

> I should not fare very well if I tried to get to the moon under my own steam, however much hardware and rocketry was put at my disposal. I should need the skilled direction of an astronaut who had done it before. Without that, I should not stand a chance. That is why Jesus said to people who turned their backs on him, "I go away, and you will seek me and die in your sins; where I am going, you cannot come" (John 8:21). Does that sound hard? Not really. You cannot get to the moon unless you commit yourself to the astronaut.[6]

Without the forgiveness that only Jesus can give, and the inward transformation of the Holy Spirit, none could stand in God's presence. There will be no place to hide our sins there. C. S. Lewis points out in *The Problem of Pain*, "The joys of Heaven are, for most of us in our present condition, 'an acquired taste'—and certain ways of life may render the taste impossible of acquisition. Perhaps the lost are those who dare not go to such a *public* place."[7]

---

4. Robertson, "Perversion, as Shown in Balaam's Character," sermon preached January 25, 1852.
5. Cited in Ford, *Good News Is for Sharing*, 34.
6. Green, *You Must Be Joking*, 131.
7. Quoted by Lewis, *Problem of Pain*, 49.

A Choice to Be Made

The eighteenth-century preacher Rowland Hill put it this way: "If an unholy man were to get into heaven, he would feel like a hog in a flower garden!"[8] And as George MacDonald said, "There is no hell with a little heaven in it—no plan to retain this or that of the devil in our hearts or our pockets. Out Satan must go, every hair and feather."[9] Nor can I take refuge in the false hope that there is some middle ground such as J. B. Priestley imagined in his book *All about Ourselves*: "As I am not good enough for heaven nor bad enough for hell, the territory in between ought not to be too disturbingly unfamiliar. So either way it ought to be all right and there is no reason why I should be afraid."[10]

If, however, I want to settle things with God for time and eternity, there is something I must *do*. It is to acknowledge my need of forgiveness, as best I know how to turn from all I know to be wrong, accept Jesus as my Savior and submit to him as the Lord of my life. If I am content to spend eternity without God, in spite of all the warnings as to what that may involve, then all I need do is—nothing! Imagine for a moment someone who has terminal cancer. As they lie on their hospital bed awaiting a certain end, a doctor comes in with some tremendous news. A drug has been discovered that can immediately reverse the effects of the cancerous cells and restore that person to health. He places a glass containing the drug by their bedside with instructions to drink it. Now, if that person is going to die, they don't have to cut their throat, or blow their brains out, or jump out the window or assault the doctor or nurse. No, all they have to do is fail to take the medicine.

We are in a similar position. Because of our sins we are in a condition the Bible describes as "perishing" (1 Cor 1:18). However, God has provided the perfect remedy for our condition in the death and resurrection of Jesus. I don't have to be a murderer, adulterer, a thief, or any "big" sinner to be lost forever. I may be the most respected citizen in town. But if I fail to come to Jesus and accept his offer, then there is no other cure for my condition. As the writer

---

8. Charlesworth, *Rowland Hill*, 224.
9. Cited by Lewis, *Great Divorce*, title page.
10. Priestley, *All about Ourselves*, 286.

Part 2: The Christian View of Life after Death

of Hebrews puts it, "How shall we escape if we ignore such a great salvation?" (Heb 2:3). It is for this reason that the Bible declares, "Everyone who does not have faith in him has already been condemned for not having faith in God's only Son" (John 3:18 CEV). The Bible also warns that by continuing to rebel against God's claim on my life through "stubbornness" and an "unrepentant heart" it is possible to *store up* "wrath against [ourselves] for the day of God's wrath, when his righteous judgment will be revealed" (Rom 2:5). However, the good news is that even if I am a "big" sinner, Jesus is able to "save completely those who come to God through him" (Heb 7:25).

And it is not enough merely to give mental assent to the truth of the gospel. "Heaven can be missed by eighteen inches," it has been said. That is the approximate distance between your head and your heart.

To quote Rowland Hill again, "Where you die—when you die—or by what means is scarcely worth a thought, if you do but die in Christ."[11]

I will finish with a delightful story told of the Christian apologist and humorist G. K. Chesterton. His eccentricities often suited the stereotype of a slovenly, absent-minded professor. He would show up at a wedding wearing no tie and with a price tag on his shoes. Using any available paper, even wallpaper, he would scribble notes when ideas came to him, sometimes standing, oblivious, in the middle of traffic as he did so. Once he sent his wife this telegram: "Am in Market Harborough. Where ought I to be?" She telegraphed back: "Home."

If you who are reading this booklet are uncertain as to where you stand in your relationship with God or your prospects for eternity, then why not come home where you belong and where you ought to be? You may find it helpful to begin by praying a prayer such as this:

> God, I accept that when you created this universe and thought of me, then you had a great purpose for me, which stretches beyond the limitations of this mortal life. Though I don't fully understand all that you may have

---

11. Quoted by Charlesworth, *Rowland Hill*, 188.

A Choice to Be Made

planned for me in this life or the next, I accept that you love me and sent Jesus to die for me in order that I might be reconciled to you and that purpose might be fulfilled.

Thank you, Jesus, for your great love.

Lord, I am coming home. I am sorry for my sins. I repent of them. I now accept your forgiveness and submit my life to Jesus as my Savior and Lord.

Come into my life and begin the process of molding me into all you planned that I should be and directing me in the path you have chosen for me.

Enable me to accept fully all that you have done for me and to be open to all that you want to do. Give me the courage and strength to live worthily of your love and to follow wherever you lead, so that when I stand before you in person I may hear those words, "My Father has blessed you! Come and receive the kingdom that was prepared for you before the world was created" (Matt 25:34 CEV).

Amen.

If you should make this kind of commitment, then dig into the New Testament which speaks not only of a glorious future for God's people, but also about how we can begin to experience some of heaven's joys in advance as we get involved with the One who planned it all. It also has much to say about how we can begin to store up treasure there in advance. Look around for others whom you can encourage on the journey also.

Teach us to number our days aright, that we may gain a heart of wisdom

—Psalm 90:12

God so loved the world that he gave his one and only Son, that whoever believes in him shall not perish but have eternal life

—John 3:16

Appendices

Included here are several poems and articles that have caught my attention over the years. The two poems, *Looking for the Sunrise* and *Treasure Up in Heaven*, and the article *A Traveller's Guide to Heaven*, I have had in my collection for many years and do not know where they first appeared in print. They are worth passing on to the next generation. The poem *Looking for the Sunrise* I have often used at funerals in my role as an Anglican pastor, and sometimes get asked for copies.

The King and the Fool appeared over sixty years ago in a small booklet titled *The Traveller's Guide from Death to Life*, which contained illustrations of the gospel compiled by Mrs. Stephen Menzies and published by the British Gospel Book Association.

Looking for the Sunrise

I'm not looking for the sunset,
As the swift years come and go;
I am looking for the sunrise,
And the golden morning glow,
Where the light of heaven's glory
Will break forth upon my sight,
In the land that knows no sunset,
Nor the darkness of the night.

I'm not going down the pathway
Toward the setting of the sun,
Where the shadows ever deepen
When the day at last is done;
I am walking up the hillside
Where the sunshine lights the way,
To the glory of the sunrise
Of God's never-ending day.

I'm not going down, but upward,
And the path is never dim,
For the day grows ever brighter
As I journey on with Him.
So my eyes are on the hilltops,
Waiting for the sun to rise,

Looking for the Sunrise

Waiting for His invitation
To the home beyond the skies.

—Albert Simpson Reitz, June 1953

Treasure Up in Heaven

You tell me I am getting old, but that's not really so.
The house I live in may be worn, and that of course I know.
It's been in use for quite a while, weathered by wind and hail.
I'm therefore not surprised to find it's getting somewhat frail!

You tell me I am getting old, you mix the house with me.
You're looking at the outside, that's all that you can see.
The dweller in this shaky house is young and bright and free;
Just starting on a life that lasts for all eternity.

The colour's changing on the roof, the window's looking dim,
The wall's a bit transparent and is getting rather thin.
The foundation's not as steady, as once it used to be;
But that is all that you observe, and really that's not me!

I patch the old house up a bit, to make it last the night,
But soon I shall be leaving for my home of endless light:
I'm going to live forever there, for life goes on—it's grand!
How can you say I'm getting old? You do not understand!

These few short years can't make me old. I feel I'm in my youth:
Eternal life is mine right now, and that's the solid truth!
I will not fret to see this house grow shabby day by day,
But look ahead to my New Home, which never will decay.

Treasure Up in Heaven

I want to be found worthy for my Father's house above;
Cleansed in the precious Blood of Christ and growing still in love.
The beauty of that glorious home no words can ever say.
'Tis hidden from these mortal eyes, but kept for me some day.

My house is getting ready in a place beyond the sky.
Its Architect and Builder is my Saviour now on high:
But He's told me that He's leaving all the furnishing to me,
So it's 'treasure up in heaven' that I'm storing—don't you see?

—Mr. L. A. T. Van Dooran

A Traveller's Guide to Heaven

Accommodation: Arrangements for first-class accommodation have been made in advance.

In my Father's house are many rooms . . . I am going there to prepare a place for you (John 14:2).

Passports: Persons seeking entry will not be permitted past the gates without having proper credentials and having their names registered with the ruling Authority.

Nothing impure will ever enter it . . . but only those whose names are written in the Lamb's book of life (Revelation 21:27).

Departure Times: The exact date of departure has not been announced. Travellers are advised to be prepared to leave at short notice.

It is not for you to know the times or the dates, which the Father has set by his own authority (Acts 1:7).

Tickets: Your ticket is a written pledge that guarantees your journey. It should be claimed and its promises kept firmly in hand.

Everyone who hears my message and has faith in the one who sent me has eternal life and will never be condemned. They have already gone from death to life (John 5:24).

A Traveller's Guide to Heaven

Customs: Only one declaration is required while going through customs.

I passed on to you as of first importance: that Christ died for our sins according to the Scriptures, that he was buried, that he was raised on the third day (1 Corinthians 15:3, 4).

Immigration: All passengers are classified as immigrants, since they are taking up permanent residence in a new country. The quota is unlimited.

They were longing for a better country—a heavenly one . . . for he has prepared a city for them (Hebrews 11:16).

Luggage: No luggage whatsoever can be taken.

We brought nothing into the world, and we can take nothing out of it (1 Timothy 6:7).

Air passage: Travellers going directly by air are advised to watch daily for indication of imminent departure.

We who are still alive and are left will be caught up, with them, in the clouds to meet the Lord in the air. And so we will be with the Lord forever (1 Thessalonians 4:17).

Vaccination and inoculation: Injections are not needed, as diseases are unknown at the destination.

He will wipe all tears from their eyes, and there will be no more death, suffering, crying, or pain. These things of the past are gone forever (Revelation 21:4).

Currency: Supplies of currency may be forwarded ahead to await the passenger's arrival. Deposits should be as large as possible.

Store up your treasures in heaven, where moths and rust cannot destroy them, and thieves cannot break in and steal them (Matthew 6:20).

Clothing: A complete and appropriate new wardrobe is provided for each traveller.

He has clothed me with garments of salvation and arrayed me in a robe of righteousness (Isaiah 61:10).

Time changes: Resetting of watches will not be necessary. Nor will the watches.

The city did not need the sun or the moon. The glory of God was shining on it, and the Lamb was its light . . . and night never comes (Revelation 21:23, 25).

Reservations: Booking is now open. Apply at once.

The time has come. This is the day for you to be saved (2 Corinthians 6:2).

Coronation ceremony: The highlight of the journey is the welcoming reception and the coronation which will await each new arrival.

There is in store for me the crown of righteousness, which the Lord, the righteous Judge, will award to me on that day—and . . . also to all who have longed for his appearing (2 Timothy 4:8).

—Marcelle Price

Heaven

The following letter was printed in a local paper some thirty years ago. It was sent to them by a parishioner of an Anglican church in Christchurch, New Zealand, whose name I do not have.

Sometime ago our Minister announced that he would be speaking the following Sunday on "Heaven." During the week a beautiful letter was received from an old man who was very ill, and the following is part of his letter. "Next Sunday you are to talk about heaven. I am very interested in that land, because I have held a clear title to a bit of property there for over 53 years. I did not buy it. It was given me without money and without price. But the Donor purchased it for me at tremendous sacrifice. I am not holding it for speculation since the title is not transferable. It is not a vacant lot. For more than half a century I have been sending materials out of which the greatest architect and builder of the Universe has been building a home for me, which will never need to be remodelled, nor repaired, because it will suit me perfectly, individually, and will never grow old. Dry rot or borer can never undermine its foundations for they rest on the 'Rock of Ages.' Fire cannot destroy it. Floods cannot wash it away. No lock or bolts will ever be placed on its doors for no evil person can ever enter that land where my dwelling stands, now almost completed, and almost ready for me to enter in and abide in peace eternally, without fear of being ejected. There is a valley of deep shadow between the place where I live in Opawa and that to which I shall journey in a very short time. I cannot reach my home in the heavenly city without passing through this dark valley of shadows. But I am not afraid because the best Friend I ever had went through the same valley long, long ago and drove away all its gloom. This Friend has stuck by me through thick and thin, since we first became acquainted 53 years ago, and I hold his promise, in printed form, never to forsake me or leave me alone. He will be with me as I walk through the valley of shadows, and I shall not lose my way when He is with me. Yes, Heaven is the centre of the Christian's universe and he is bound to it by 8 golden links. 1) Our Father is there (Matthew 6:9). 2) Our Saviour is there (Hebrews 9:24). 3) Our home is there (John 14:2–4). 4) Our name is there (Luke 10:20). 5) Our life is there (Colossians 3:1–3). 6) Our heart is there (Matthew 6:19–21). 7) Our inheritance is there (1 Peter 1:3–5). 8) Our citizenship is there (Philippians 3:20). Yes, this old man is ready to travel there, are you? A man may go to heaven without wealth, without health, without fame, without a great name, without learning, without money, without culture, without beauty, without friends, without 10,000 other things. But he can never go to heaven without having accepted Jesus Christ as his Saviour and Lord in this life."

Hamish

This poem is my own hesitant effort at writing poetry. I composed it on the occasion of the memorial service for our little grandson who died in his mother's womb at seven and a half months.

> In sorrow and with heavy hearts
> We gather on this day,
> To cast to earth a little lad,
> To share, to grieve, to pray.
> For little Hamish, ere he knew
> To either laugh or cry,
> Was taken from us suddenly,
> And now we wonder why.
> That hand that never held a spade,
> That eye that never saw,
> Those feet that never trod the soil,
> Now seem to be no more.
>
> But this is only part the tale,
> For we have hope above—
> A God with power beyond this world
> Whose character is Love;
> A God who knows the depths of pain,
> In Person of his Son
> Took human nature, flesh and blood—
> For us the victory won.

Hamish

He lived through hunger, thirst and trial,
He knew both joy and gloom,
He prayed through many sleepless hours,
He wept at Lazarus' tomb.
Through death he plumbed the depths of hell,
In power he rose to reign,
And demonstrated once for all
A final end to pain.

And so, in faith we journey on,
We trust, if cannot see,
In hope of glory yet to come,
Touched by eternity.
And when at last the trumpet sounds,
And this grey sleeping dust
Is transformed by God's mighty power,
Then he will rise with us.
In instant recognition then
No stranger will we meet—
A loving son, a friend in Christ—
A family complete.
Then we shall see what traits, what gifts,
Within your genes were sealed,
What personality is yours,
In manhood full revealed.
So, Hamish, though we still do grieve,
We follow where we're led;
And till that glorious break of Day
We send our love ahead.

—Dick Tripp, 15 October 1998

The King and the Fool

A certain lord kept a fool, or jester, in his house, as great men did in olden times for their amusement. His lord gave a staff to his fool, and charged him to keep it until he met with a greater fool than himself, and if he met with such a one, to deliver it over to him. Not many years after, the lord fell sick. His fool came to see him, and was told of his master's illness. "And where will you go?" asked the fool. "On a long journey," said the lord. "And when will you come again? Within a month?" "No," said his master. "Within a year?" "No." "What then—never?" "Never." "And what provision have you made for where you are going?" "None at all." "Are you going away for ever," said the fool, "and have made no provision before your departure? Here, take my staff, for I am not guilty of any such folly as that."

From *The Traveller's Guide from Death to Life*, compiled by Mrs. Stephen Menzies, published by the British Gospel Book Association.

Will You Meet Me at the Fountain?

There is an old Sankey hymn, "Will You Meet Me at the Fountain?" It was written at the time of a great Industrial Exhibition in Chicago and "the fountain" was the place where everybody arranged to meet their friends. It expresses my wish for you, the reader of this booklet:

> Will you meet me at the Fountain
> When I reach the glory land
> Will you meet me at the Fountain
> Shall I clasp your friendly hand?
> Other friends will give me welcome,
> Other loving voices cheer,
> There'll be music at the Fountain,
> Will you meet me there?
>
> Will you meet me at the Fountain?
> I shall long to have you near
> When I meet my loving Saviour,
> When His welcome words I hear.
> He will meet me at the Fountain,
> His embraces I shall share.
> There'll be glory at the Fountain,
> Will you, will you meet me there?

Bibliography

Adams, Moody. *The Titanic's Last Hero.* West Columbia, SC: Olive, 1997.
Anderson, Norman. *Christianity and the World Religions: The Challenge of Pluralism.* London: InterVarsity, 1984.
Barr, James. *Biblical Words for Time.* Naperville, IL: Allenson, 1962.
Bavinck, Herman. *Gereformeerde Dogmatiek.* 3rd ed. Vol. 4. 1918. Translated into English as *Reformed Dogmatics* by John Vriend. Edited by John Bolt. Grand Rapids: Baker Academic, 2008.
Baxter, Richard. *Poetical Fragments: Heart-Imployment with God and It Self, the Concordant Discord of a Broken-healed Heart.* London, 1689.
Bayly, Joseph. *The View from the Hearse.* Colorado Springs: Cook, 1969.
Becker, Ernest. *The Denial of Death.* New York: Free Press, 1997.
Bevan, Edwyn. *Symbolism and Belief.* London: Allen & Unwin, 1938.
Blackham, Harold J., ed. *Objections to Humanism.* Philadelphia: Lippincott, 1965.
Bonar, Andrew A. *Heavenly Springs: Portions for the Sabbaths of a Year.* London, 1886.
Boreham, F. W. *The Prodigal: Sidelights on an Immortal Story.* London: Epworth, 1941.
Bourne, F. W. *Billy Bray: The King's Son.* London: Epworth, 1949.
Bray, Wendy. *In the Palm of God's Hand.* Oxford: Bible Reading Fellowship, 2007.
Brunner, Emil. *Man in Revolt.* 1st English translation by Olive Wyon. London: Lutterworth, 1939.
Bryan, William Jennings. *The Prince of Peace.* New York: Revell, 1909.
Bull, Geoffrey T. *When Iron Gates Yield.* London: Hodder & Stoughton, 1957.
Bunyan, John. *Grace Abounding to the Chief of Sinners: A Brief and Faithful Relation of the Exceeding Mercy of God. . . .* London, 1666.
Caldwell, Louis O. *Another Tassel Is Moved: Guidelines for College Graduates.* Grand Rapids: Baker, 1977.
Carey, George. *The Gate of Glory.* London: Hodder & Stoughton, 1986.
Chapman, Colin. *The Case for Christianity.* Tring, UK: Lion, 1981.

Bibliography

Charlesworth, Vernon J. *Rowland Hill: His Life, Anecdotes and Pulpit Sayings.* London, 1882.

Chignell, Peter. *Set Free and Now a Prisoner.* Christchurch, New Zealand: Outreach Press, 1992.

Dale, R. W. *The Atonement: The Congregational Union Lecture for 1875.* London, 1894.

Day, Richard Ellsworth. *The Shadow of the Broad Brim: The Story of Charles Haddon Spurgeon.* Philadelphia: Judson, 1949.

Deems, Edward M. *Holy-Days and Holidays: A Treasury of Historical Material.* . . . New York: Funk & Wagnalls, 1906.

Donne, John. *The Works of John Donne: With a Memoir of His Life by Henry Alford.* Vol. 4. London: Parker, 1839.

Douglas, J. D., ed. *The New Bible Dictionary.* London: InterVarsity, 1962.

Drummond, Henry. *The Greatest Thing in the World.* London, 1890.

Dudley-Smith, Timothy. *John Stott: A Global Ministry.* Leicester, UK: InterVarsity, 2001.

Edwards, David L., and John R. W. Stott. *Essentials: A Liberal-Evangelical Dialogue.* London: Hodder & Stoughton, 1988.

Elliot, Elisabeth. *Keep a Quiet Heart.* Ann Arbor: Servant, 1995.

Evans, A. R. *Dan Crawford.* 2nd ed. Grand Rapids: Zondervan, 1959.

Fee, Gordon. *God's Empowering Presence: The Holy Spirit in the Letters of St. Paul.* Peabody, MA: Hendrickson, 1994.

Fiske, John. *The Destiny of Man, Viewed in the Light of His Origin.* London, 1890. Available online at http://www.forgottenbooks.com/books/The_Destiny_of_Man_1000289403.

Fitt, Arthur P. *The Shorter Life of D. L. Moody.* Chicago: Moody, 1900.

Fleming, Robert. *The Fulfilling of Scripture.* 1801.

Ford, Leighton. *Good News Is for Sharing.* Colorado Springs: Cook, 1977.

Frazer, James George. *The Belief in Immortality and the Worship of the Dead.* Vol. 1. London: Macmillan, 1913.

Friedman, Howard, ed. *Encyclopedia of Mental Health.* Vol. 2. New York: Academic, 1998.

Glegg, A. Lindsay. *Four Score. . .and More: Some Pages from My Scrapbook.* Edinburgh: Marshall, Morgan & Scott, 1962.

Gordon, Margaret M. *The Home Life of Sir David Brewster: By His Daughter Mrs. Gordon.* Edinburgh, 1870.

Graham, Billy. *Death and the Life After.* Nashville: Nelson, 1994.

———. *World Aflame.* New York: Doubleday, 1965.

Green, Michael. *Man Alive!* Leicester, UK: InterVarsity, 1967.

———. *The Meaning of Salvation.* Vancouver: Regent College Press, 2000.

———. *Runaway World.* London: InterVarsity, 1968.

———. *You Must Be Joking: Popular Excuses for Avoiding Jesus Christ.* London: Hodder & Stoughton, 1991. First published 1976.

Grubb, Norman P. *After C. T. Studd.* London: Lutterworth, 1946. First published 1939.

BIBLIOGRAPHY

———. *C. T. Studd*. London: Lutterworth, 1957. First published 1953.
Guinness, Os. *The Dust of Death: A Critique of the Establishment and the Counter Culture*. Wheaton: Crossway, 1973.
Havergal, Maria V. G. *Memorials of Francis Ridley Havergal*. London, 1880.
Helm, Paul. *The Last Things*. London: Banner of Truth, 1989.
Hendriksen, William. *The Bible on the Life Hereafter*. Grand Rapids: Baker, 1975. First published 1959.
Hennell, Michael. *John Venn and the Clapham Sect*. London: Lutterworth, 1958.
Houghton, William H. "By Life, or By Death." Hymn d275, in *Voice of Thanksgiving*, vol. 5. Chicago: Moody, 1946.
Huegel, F. J. *The Cross through the Scriptures*. Minneapolis: Bethany Fellowship, 1966.
Hunt, Gladys M. *The Christian Way of Death*. Grand Rapids: Zondervan, 1971.
Kelsey, Morton. *Encounter with God*. London: Hodder & Stoughton, 1972.
Klassen, Randolph. *What Does the Bible Really Say about Hell? Wrestling with the Traditional View*. Telford, PA: Pandora, 2001.
Koop, C. Everett, and Francis A. Schaeffer. *Whatever Happened to the Human Race?* Westchester, IL: Crossway, 1983.
Kreeft, Peter. *Heaven: The Heart's Deepest Longing*. San Francisco: Ignatius, 1993.
———. *Making Sense out of Suffering*. Cincinnati: Servant, 1986.
Lewis, C. S. *The Four Loves*. Glasgow: Collins, 1977.
———. *The Great Divorce*. London: Bles, 1945.
———. *The Last Battle*. New York: HarperCollins, 1956.
———. *Letters to Malcolm*. New York: Harcourt Brace Jovanovich, 1963.
———. *Mere Christianity*. Glasgow: Collins, 1986.
———. *The Problem of Pain*. Glasgow: Collins, 1986.
Longfellow, Henry Wadsworth. *Hyperion: A Romance*. New York, 1839.
Macpherson, Ian. *The Punctuality of God*. Hollis, NH: Puritan, 1946.
Marsh, John W., and Waite H. Stirling. *The Story of Commander Allen Gardiner, R.N.* London, 1883.
McDonald, George. *Mary Marston*. The Literature Network. http://www.online-literature.com/george-macdonald/mary-marston.
McGrath, Alister. *Suffering*. London: Hodder & Stoughton, 1992.
Moody, D. L. *Finding God*. Chicago: Moody, 1958.
———. *The Gospel Awakening*. Edited by L. T. Remlap. Chicago, 1885.
Moule, H. C. G. *Charles Simeon*. London: InterVarsity, 1948.
———. *Harriot Mary Moule: A Short Memorial for Her Friends*. Durham, UK: privately printed, 1915.
———. *Second Epistle to Timothy*. London: Religious Tract Society, 1905.
Neff, David. "Honest Appraisal: Learning from Reformers, Past and Present." *Christianity Today*, October 1, 2010. http://www.christianitytoday.com/ct/2010/october/4.5.html.
Nicholls, Bruce. *Is Jesus the Only Way to God?* Auckland: Affirm, 1998.

BIBLIOGRAPHY

O'Neill, Eugene. *Long Day's Journey into Night*. New Haven: Yale University Press, 1956.
Packer, J. I. *God's Plans for You*. Wheaton: Crossway, 2001.
———. *Great Joy: A 31-Day Devotional*. Compiled by Beth N. Feia. Ann Arbor: Vine, 1998.
———. *Knowing God*. London: Hodder & Stoughton, 1973.
———. *A Quest for Godliness: The Puritan Vision of the Christian Life*. Wheaton: Crossway, 1990.
Pascal, Blaise. *Pensées*. 1669.
Paton, John G. *John G. Paton: Missionary to the New Hebrides*. Edited by James Paton. London, 1884.
Pollock, John. *Amazing Grace: John Newton's Story*. London: Hodder & Stoughton, 1981.
Post, Stephen G., and Robert H. Binstock, eds. *The Fountain of Youth: Cultural, Scientific and Ethical Perspectives on a Biomedical Goal*. New York: Oxford University Press, 2004.
Priestley, J. B. *All about Ourselves, and Other Essays*. London, 1956.
Purves, Jock. *Fair Sunshine*. Rev. ed. Edinburgh: Banner of Truth, 1968. Originally published as two works: *Sweet Believing*, 1948; and *Fair Sunshine*, 1957.
Rawnsley, C. F., and Robert Wright. *Night Fighter*. London: Ballantyne, 1998.
Reece, Richard. *Compendious Martyrology*. Vol. 3. London, 1815.
Rees, Jean. *His Name Was Tom: The Biography of Tom Rees*. London: Hodder & Stoughton, 1971.
Ross, Hugh. *Beyond the Cosmos*. Colorado Springs: NavPress, 1996.
Ryle, J. C. *The Christian Leaders of England in the Eighteenth Century*. London, 1863.
Shea, George Beverly. *Then Sings My Soul*. London: Hodder & Stoughton, 1968.
Skinner, Betty Lee. *Daws: The Story of Dawson Trotman*. Grand Rapids: Zondervan, 1974.
Snodgrass, Klyne. *Between Two Truths: Living with Biblical Tensions*. Eugene, OR: Wipf & Stock, 2004.
Speake, Jennifer, ed. *Oxford Dictionary of Proverbs*. 5th ed. Oxford: Oxford University Press, 2008.
Spurgeon, Charles H. *Spurgeon's Sermons on Death and Resurrection of Jesus*. Peabody, MA: Hendrickson, 2005.
Stott, John R. W. *Christ the Liberator: Urbana 70*. Downers Grove: InterVarsity, 1971.
———. *Christian Mission in the Modern World*. London: Falcon, 1975.
———. *The Incomparable Christ*. Based on the AD 2000 London Lectures in Contemporary Christianity. Leicester, UK: InterVarsity, 2001.
Tada, Joni Eareckson. *Heaven: Your Real Home*. Grand Rapids: Zondervan, 1995.
Temple, William. *Nature, Man and God*. Gifford Lectures. New York: AMS, 1934.

BIBLIOGRAPHY

Tillich, Paul. *The Shaking of the Foundations*. New York: Scribner, 1948.

Tozer, A. W. *The Knowledge of the Holy: The Attributes of God, Their Meaning in the Christian Life*. London: Clarke, 1965.

———. *Who Put Jesus on the Cross? And Other Questions of the Christian Faith*. Camp Hill, PA: Christian Publications, 1976.

Twelftree, Graham. *Drive the Point Home*. Crowborough, UK: Monarch, 1994.

Watson, David. *Fear No Evil*. Wheaton: Shaw, 1884.

White, Edward. *Life in Christ: A Study of the Scripture Doctrine on the Nature of Man, the Object of the Divine Incarnation, and the Conditions of Human Immortality*. London, 1878.

White, Ellen G. *The Great Controversy between Christ and Satan*. Oakland, 1858.

Whiting, Nathan. *The Works of That Eminent Servant of Christ, John Bunyan*. New Haven, 1831.

Winter, David. *Hereafter: A New Look at an Old Question; What Happens after Death?* London: Hodder & Stoughton, 1972.

Wurmbrand, Richard. *Tortured for Christ*. Bartlesville, OK: Living Sacrifice, 1998.

Yancey, Philip. *I Was Just Wondering*. Grand Rapids: Eerdmans, 1998.

———. *The Jesus I Never Knew*. Sydney: Strand, 2000.

Zacharias, Ravi. *A Shattered Visage: The Real Face of Atheism*. Grand Rapids: Baker, 1993.

www.ingramcontent.com/pod-product-compliance
Lightning Source LLC
Chambersburg PA
CBHW070911160426
43193CB00011B/1425